Praise

Outsource Your ~~Book~~

Like many entrepreneurs I'd love to have a book out but I wouldn't even know where to start! *Wall Street Journal* bestselling author Alinka Rutkowska shows you exactly where to go to outsource each of the 17 steps to creating and launching a bestselling book. She even lists the investment necessary to complete each step. While I found *Outsource Your Book* to be extremely informative, it's also overwhelming to think of everything that needs to be done to create a bestseller. I'll just hire Rutkowska's publishing company, Leaders Press to take it off my plate!

– **Ali Razi** |
Founder & CEO, Banc Certified Merchant Services

There are big projects in life that someone can manage themselves, if they choose, and outsource each component. One that comes to mind is building a house. You can operate as a general contractor, and hire a separate architect, foundation company, mechanical/electrical/plumbing, framing, drywall, flooring and many other needed trade professionals. Writing and publishing a book requires many subcontractors to produce a bestseller. Interviewing, writing, editing, book cover, publishing, reviews, marketing, etc. all require separate skill sets. If each component, just like when building a house, is not carefully managed, the end product will suffer or even fail. In any endeavor, it is always the "You don't know what you don't know" areas that bite you. This book outlines exactly how to make sure you don't fall into that trap.

– **Allen Sanders** |
Financial Strategist and Founder of Empowerment Concepts

If you are thinking about writing a book, save yourself time and money by carefully reviewing this very concise guide on how best to leave your legacy behind in words. After working with several publishers as well as self-publishing a total of eight books myself, I still learned so much! An invaluable resource.

– **Joe Dinoffer** | President, OnCourt OffCourt

I have tremendous praise for Alinka and her team, having been through the book-writing process with them from soup to nuts. Simply put, if you want to create a bestselling book, use Leaders Press. If you want to write a book and hope for the best, then do that instead. Alinka and her team are professional, competent, courteous, passionate and attentive. I will use her team again when it's time to write my second bestselling book!

– **David Fuess** |
CEO Catapult Systems and bestselling author
of *Why They Buy*

Outsource Your Book

Your Guide to Getting Your Business Book Ghostwritten, Published and Launched

Alinka Rutkowska

Leaders
Press

Leaders
Press

Share your knowledge. It is a way to achieve immortality. —Dalai Lama XIV

Contents

INTRODUCTION

Why You Need This Book

Congratulations on wanting to outsource your book! You already know that your time is better spent running your business.

While you're a respected business leader and expert, many people throughout the world aren't aware of your knowledge. You've been thinking about how valuable your life lessons would be to others, and leaving a legacy is one of your deepest desires.

There are many things you want to accomplish; the question is how or what is the best way to do it.

The short answer is with a book.

Naturally, though, you're busy. Where would you find the time to write an entire book?

The easy answer is to outsource your book.

Hire professionals to do it for you! It's easier than you might think.

Allow me to throw out a few more reasons why you should hire out for your book:

- ❑ authority — establishes you as the expert in your arena;
- ❑ visibility — customers, CEOs, business people around the world will know who you are;

- ❑ credibility — a book is the new calling card for your company;
- ❑ financial — a properly marketed book is a cash-generating asset (Yes, even one book!);
- ❑ invitation — top-ranked books provide many readers with an entrance into your world;
- ❑ popularity — books open the door to speaking gigs;
- ❑ consultancy — to be a consultant in semi-retirement, a book is a perfect method to get there;
- ❑ legacy — explain to your family and heirs just what you did when you were not at home;
- ❑ ease — all of the above just happens without you having to write the book yourself!

A book that is appropriately and cleverly marketed is a powerful way to increase your visibility. Millions of people have access to books through a variety of channels, such as online through Amazon or in person at the local library. Additionally, foreign publishers, including those in China (which is a huge market), are seeking new books to introduce to their markets. That naturally increases your exposure among leaders.

As an expert, your book is your ultimate business card. Nothing increases your authority in the eyes of your customers, employees and strangers as much as being a published author, particularly a bestselling author.

With that said, most books struggle to sell more than a few hundred copies. All that work for nothing? Why don't they sell?

Read on to discover the magic.

At Leaders Press, we take care of everything for you. **Go to outsourcemybook.com to have us take you and your book idea under our wing**, but let me walk you through the steps if you want to outsource every single domino separately. I'm not sure if you've done any research on Leaders Press or me, but I want to let you know that as a Top 100 bestselling business author, I've sold more than 100,000 books and I've launched all Leaders Press books to bestseller status.

Leaders Press is a *USA Today* and *Wall Street Journal* bestselling press, and our process has been featured in *Entrepreneur* magazine, so you're in great company when you collaborate with us. Go to leaderspress.com, and you'll see exactly what type of results we're able to deliver and the kind of authors (usually presidents and CEOs of companies) who work with us.

Now let's get started!

CHAPTER 1

Positioning

It's important to start your book-writing process with the end goal in mind. Ask yourself what success will look like for you. In most instances, the key to success is finding an uncrowded niche. One of the top reasons I see that authors fail to meet their goals is because they did not identify a category where their book could simultaneously *fit in* and *stand out*. Yes, believe it or not, something so simple can make or break your book; can determine whether it will be a bestseller.

With my book *How I Sold 80,000 Books*, I *fit in* to the book-marketing niche by answering a fundamental question (how to sell more books) while also *standing out* with my approach using the 4Ps marketing-mix framework

- ❑ product
- ❑ place
- ❑ price
- ❑ promotion.

While you're thinking about how to write a book, it may seem like you're putting the cart before the horse, but it's time to consider what will sell as you lay out your plan. How do you come up with a book idea and content that will be the entry to your six-figure funnel?

I'm going to share a big secret and a couple of short case studies to illustrate what this looks like.

Secret: Fit In and Stand Out

To be successful, the book has to *fit in* and *stand out*.

What does that mean exactly?

Case Study No. 1: my fiction series called **Maya and Filippo** — a series of adventure stories of two children who travel the world on a cruise ship

How does this book series *fit in*?

There are other picture books on travel. That's good as it means there is demand, and that the books sell, so there is already an established, lucrative niche. Your book has to *fit in* to an existing niche; however, it also has to have a unique selling proposition so that it will *stand out*.

How does this book series *stand out*?

While there are picture books on travel, there was no cruise-ship approach, so this is the first such concept for children's books, and that's excellent. This unique selling proposition opened the doors to foreign rights and bulk sales, which I will discuss later on. Believe me, as you launch your book and promote it far and wide, those foreign publishers are watching for hot new concepts. Publishers are continually looking for new material, and in countries, such as China, the vast majority of the books they publish come from abroad. This means they might be looking for your book if you position it correctly.

I recently received a message with the subject line "Thai Translation Rights for *Write and Grow Rich*". It was from an agent in Thailand, asking if the Thai foreign rights for one of my more recent releases were available. I connected them with my foreign-rights agent (who handles these things for me). I'll talk more about that later.

Case Study No. 2: my book *Supreme Leadership*, launched in January 2018

How does this book *fit in*?

First, there are other books on leadership, naturally, as leadership is a very competitive category. It might be counterintuitive to say that's good — because you might be tempted to think it means that the horizon is too crowded. Competitive categories mean that people are interested, so I launched another book on leadership.

I'll give you a piece of advice here, as you can't just launch a copycat book into competitive arenas; you have to *stand out*.

How does this book *stand out*?

To create it, my team and I interviewed 34 CEOs who were celebrating 25 years in business that year. It, therefore, *stood out* as no one had done something like that before.

Incidentally, this book became an entry to another six-figure funnel of mine, and I'll tell you how that works in a bit. One thing at a time!

Case Study No. 3: another one of my recent releases, *Write and Grow Rich*, showing authors how they can turn their books into a six-figure calling

There were other books on book marketing, one of which was mine. I knew that there was demand for this type of know-how, so it was quite easy to *fit in* to that market.

How did our book *stand out?*

Instead of being about 34 CEOs, this book was written by 24 experts on writing. While the interest in the subject matter was there, there was no 24-expert approach before our book's release. I hadn't seen anything like that done before, which was good for us. That was our unique selling proposition.

This book is an entry point to the funnel of every one of the 24 authors because each author has a link in the book. Once somebody clicks, they can follow up with the co-author, and can sign up for their list.

You must be saying, "Well, good for them, but what about me?"

Here's another example. An author came to me, and although I could see she had potential, there was room for improvement in both the writing and marketing of her Young Adult fiction featuring cats. So we completely repositioned her book by changing her conventional narrative into the form of a diary.

Even though there were other diaries — that's good as it means it *fits in* — there were no diaries featuring cats — that's good because it *stands out*. The last time I checked, this book had a high ranking. In addition, she's working with my foreign-rights agent, because after the book was repositioned, my foreign-rights agent took an interest in it. (We will discuss foreign-rights acquisition in a later chapter.)

Case Study No. 4: *Pocket Mentor*, created by Leaders Press for the CEO of a grill-manufacturing company

The book did so well that it overtook my own book in the bestseller charts!

There were other books on leadership, but there was no mentor-plus-mastermind approach. The unique selling proposition here is that when you get this book, it's like having a mentor in your pocket. In addition, there's a mastermind connected to it, so you can get the author to interact with you and help you with your business. That's yet another selling point that we created.

Why They Buy, a book we created for the CEO of an IT consultancy, is another example of *fitting in* and *standing out*. There were other books on sales (great!), but there was no book about effectively closing the sale in the digital realm. As you might expect by now, we launched it to the top of the bestseller charts.

Case Study No. 5: this very publication, *Outsource Your Book*

There already is a market for books on book writing and book marketing (great!), but nobody has ever done a book on how you can outsource your book! That's its unique selling proposition. Perhaps you think that it's all been done before. Well, no, as you see, it hasn't.

There's a saying that everything that could be invented has already been invented. Well, you wouldn't be reading this book if that was true. Even though there are millions and millions of books, not everything has been done yet; not every approach has been taken; not every subject matter has been discussed; not every packaging and marketing approach has been used.

You can, therefore, come up with a unique selling proposition that no one else has done before.

If you think that because you already have a book out there, it's too late for you, think again. You can always reposition, repackage, and remarket your book.

Where to outsource positioning

This is a tricky one because it requires vast knowledge of the market in your particular genre. I'm confident to say that most of the authors whom I invited to be co-authors of *Write and Grow Rich* should be able to help. Their details are given at the back of the book.

Cost

This could probably be done in a 60-minute strategy call = approximate cost $600.

CHAPTER 2

Outline

Your book's outline may be the most challenging step in the process, believe it or not.

You might think that coming up with, dictating, or writing 40-60,000 words in your book would be the step to bog you down, but it's not. Figuring out the concept behind what to include in your book is the crucial first step. The rest is cake!

If I can make a simple analogy, let's say you want to have a home built for your family. You're going to put the most work in up-front, aren't you? Think of all the steps you'll need to take before the build even starts. You hire an architect to create the design you want. You determine how much square footage you want and can afford. You consider where to put in the windows and doors. Then you must think about things such as power, heating and cooling. Lastly, there are the floors and the roof to consider. Many decisions need to be made to figure out the frame and design of your new home.

A book requires a similar set of steps.

- ❏ You hire a professional.
- ❏ You figure out the ideal word count.
- ❏ You think about these aspects:
  - ✓ flow;
  - ✓ concept;
  - ✓ editing;
  - ✓ layout;

- ✓ formatting;
- ✓ cover;
- ✓ description;
- ✓ positioning.

Sound intimidating?

It really isn't (if you hire the right architect and builders, i.e. the right publishing professionals).

To outsource the outline — just like with hiring the best architect — it's best to speak with someone knowledgeable in your genre's book arena. You can place an ad and hire a ghostwriter that you can attempt to find at freelancing sites that I mention at the end of this chapter.

These types of outsourcing sites are full of working professionals in the online world. Their talents and skills and experience range widely all over the spectrum, from beginners to experts.

With so many choices, your challenge will be to sift through the possibilities, and then hire the right ghostwriter for your outline.

Here are some seasoned words of advice: while the ghostwriter is indispensable, you can't expect that she will position, publish, and launch the book too!

(I can promise that you will find many applicants who will say they will write, publish, market, and launch your book.)

Don't fall for it!

Ghostwriters are experts at writing a stellar product — the good ones at least — but you will need an entirely different set of skills to launch your book. Writing and marketing are not the same things (more on that later).

Here's another tip from the bucket of the deep well of industry knowledge: there are typically two categories of writers. Some writers consider themselves pantsers, meaning they write by the seat of their pants. The other writers are plotters, meaning they plan or outline their writing. (I believe in planning because it's easier to engage your reader and to convince them to take action if you know the result you want to achieve in the end.)

The next step in the process is as the transcriptions roll-in. Your ghostwriter will begin crafting them into your manuscript. When interviewing ghostwriters, ask candidates to provide work samples so you can get a sense of their style. Just like with any form of art, writing is very subjective and every artist has a different flair.

Some will write your manuscript while sticking to exactly what you say — and some authors like it to be "just so". Other writers will do research, add in quotes from others, and add context to your manuscript. There is also the entire reworking of the manuscripts into a fresh, new perspective of your content.

There most definitely is no one-size-fits-all when it comes to writers, which can make your choice a little challenging. Since you're choosing a writer before you've even written your book, how do you choose the right one to fit your vision?

And — oh my — what if you don't have a vision yet? What if all you have is an idea or a concept?

Don't panic. I've been doing this for a while, so I have the advice you need.

My process is to outsource a chapter to a couple of different writers. I suggest you pick anywhere from two to three, provide them with a transcript of a section, and see what they can do. I call these test drives, which is having part of your transcript written by two or three different ghostwriters to see which style you prefer. Aside from style preference, you're going to want to choose a ghostwriter with whom you feel comfortable working. It's essential to have a good relationship because you'll be spending a lot of time together to craft your story. In addition to the art of their writing, you'll want to be comfortable with their way of asking questions, their listening style and how the two of you get along together. This is every bit as important as their writing talent and style!

Sounds like you're looking for a needle in a haystack? It's not as challenging as it seems. Talented, seasoned ghostwriters are worth their weight in gold. They know how to step back and focus on you. They allow you to shine. They take a very active interest in your story to ensure they get all the relevant information they feel readers will want to learn from you. They have experience in approaching your story both from the helicopter view and the granular level. They understand that details matter just as much as the overall structure. Be sure to hire a ghostwriter who understands all of the above.

You'll want the writer to adapt their writing style to your preferences, so the book sounds like you. As I mentioned above, different authors want different styles. If you know you want your words written in a certain way — either just as you lay them down or artfully crafted — be sure to speak up right away.

As the interviews click along, your story will take shape. You can expect your ghostwriter to work closely with you and keep you in the loop as your story progresses. This is generally accomplished one chapter at a time.

You may be invited to view the work in progress on Google Drive, so you see the book written in real time. You may prefer to receive chapters by email to read and evaluate. Some authors choose (and may not have the time to do otherwise) to see the completed first draft before reading and becoming involved.

In summary, when choosing your ghostwriter have the following questions in mind:

1) How will interviews take place?

2) Who will do the transcriptions?

3) How will my words be edited? (Direct words or re-write of my thoughts?)

4) How well would we work together?

5) Am I comfortable discussing my information with this writer?

6) How will I receive the work in progress? By Google Drive? By email? And how often?

Let's say you have found your ideal ghostwriter. Your first step together will be to come up with an outline.

I'm sure you've read many books, so you are no doubt aware of what I'm going to say next, although you may not be aware that you are already in the know.

In its purest form, the bones of the outline should include:

- ❑ title
- ❑ dedication
- ❑ introduction
- ❑ Chapter 1
- ❑ Chapter 2
- ❑ continuing chapters
- ❑ conclusion
- ❑ acknowledgments
- ❑ appendices/bibliography/index (if required).

Within the outline, however — just as how your architect will build in space for your furniture and living environment— your ghostwriter will build in space for the following:

- ❑ a 'hook' that is so fascinating that the readers continue to read on;
- ❑ a 25 percent point of no return;
- ❑ a 50 percent midpoint;
- ❑ a 75 percent point;
- ❑ a satisfying ending (and a call to action).

Like viewers of movies and TV programs, readers are wired to expect something big to happen at 25, 50 and 75 percent of the way through books. You may not have noticed these pre-planned points before — but you will now!

Now that you've given some thought to the outline, and learned that this is the time when you need to consider how to *fit in* and how to *stand out* — let's move on to getting the ideas out of your head.

Where to outsource an outline

Credo

Fiverr

FreeeUp

Freelancer

Hubstaff Talent

Outsourcely

PeoplePerHour

Textbroker

Upwork

Workhoppers

Cost

With an experienced ghostwriter and some ideas of your own, you should be able to put it together in 90 minutes. The approximate cost of interviewing time, transcription and writing is $500.

CHAPTER 3

Getting the Ideas out of Your Head

Now that you've completed the outline of your bestseller with the help of your trusted ghostwriter, it's time to get the ideas out of your head and create your first draft.

I know you've undoubtedly watched this scene in many, many movies: a (usually) bespectacled, burned-out writer stares at a computer screen with shoulders slumped.

The cursor blinks.

The writer blinks.

And blinks.

And blinks...

Perhaps you've even experienced the dreaded 'writer's block' stare before. Well, that's not going to be your problem when you outsource your book! You don't have to stare at a white screen, and figure out what to write. Your ghostwriter (and others) will take care of that whole process for you.

Whew!

Consider that the average adult typing speed is 38 to 40 words per minute; however, the average speaking rate is more than three times faster at 130 words per minute. Instead of spending years writing your book, you can complete your book in just a couple of months through interviews or recording it yourself.

I highly suggest an interviewer for this process. That is often, but doesn't have to be, your ghostwriter.

You have some idea of what you imagine your book will be. Perhaps it's business advice; lessons learned; a focus on your specific line of work; a legacy piece; or a book of your achievements for your heirs. That's a topic you will have broadly touched upon with your ghostwriter as you worked together to prepare your outline.

Now, how do you get your words out of your head and onto the page? What if you're not a natural speaker? What if you're not sure what to say? What if it isn't easy for you to convey what you want to say to others; what if you have an idea in your head but you don't know how to turn it into a book? What if you're a 'rambler'? What if you say "like" or "you know" or "right?" when you speak? Well, don't panic. Take a deep breath and relax. This part is very easy.

Just like that blank computer screen, those concerns aren't your problems. You will answer questions, and someone else will take care of all that pesky editing. (Lucky you!)

One of the best things you can do when preparing your draft is to have someone else interview you. Based on the interviewer's questions, this exercise can also help you and your writer identify any topics you need to flesh out.

Say you want to deliver information like "I went to Harvard and almost flunked out the first semester."

An interviewer won't let you get away with that statement. They will likely ask, "What happened? Which class? Did you seek out mentoring or join a study group? How did you get back on track and graduate near the top of your class? What did you learn from your easy failure? How did you feel about yourself?"

If you say, "During the last recession, the business almost folded. We had let our staff go, and my partner and I worked 12-hour days to keep the doors open. We answered the phones. We packaged our product. We drove it to the post office to ship it ourselves." You might think that's a complete answer; however, when you're telling your story to others, they will have questions. They will want to know things you may not have considered.

Your interviewer might ask, "Did you ever hire your staff back? Did you hire the same staff or new staff? How long did it take you before you were back on your feet and turning a profit? Did you take substantial salary cuts? How did this affect your families? Did you have to give anything up on the personal side to keep the business afloat?"

You might not think of specific details to include, but during your conversations, your interviewer will.

At this point, you have considered the examples I provided in the previous chapter. You have some idea of the market where your book will be competing. You know if there is a category, such as successful architects, and that's what you're going to discuss, readers already want what you have to offer.

You just have to write it. Correction: you just have to have it written.

As an exercise, let's say Brian Tracy is writing a book about his successful architectural career. He's designed some notable buildings. People like what he does. He commands an enviable salary. He didn't, however, become a success overnight, did he? Of course not. He had an idea of what he wanted to do. He learned how to design (in this instance, he went to college, but not all entrepreneurs do). He started a business. He convinced clients to hire him. His designs were built. He became a name. People look at the skyline and say, "Wow! Brian Tracy must have designed that building! I can tell by the purple turrets!"

That's the synopsis, of course, but there's a lot of space there for an interviewer to ask questions and bring his history, ethos and personality to life.

Let's return to the outline for a moment:

- ❑ title
- ❑ dedication
- ❑ introduction
- ❑ Chapter 1
- ❑ Chapter 2
- ❑ continuing chapters
- ❑ conclusion
- ❑ acknowledgments
- ❑ appendices/bibliography/index (if required)

You may have a title in mind already, but if not, that's okay. Your dedication and acknowledgments may come later, after you've worked through your book and realized how influential certain people have been in your life.

In an introduction, you tell readers the purpose of the book and how that purpose is to be fulfilled. In the last chapter, we learned the introduction will have a hook that is so fascinating that the readers continue reading.

Let's return to our architect, Brian Tracy. To get the hook, his interviewer could ask, "What's the one piece of advice you would offer young architects seeking to emulate your career path?" He could then ask additional questions, such as "What was the defining moment that made you a fan of architecture?", "What's different now from the time when you started your career?" and "What advice would you offer to young people in school considering becoming an architect?" You get the point.

While you probably have the 100ft. view of your book (but it's okay if you don't have it yet), your interviewer won't know anything about your expertise or your specialty or your struggles and achievements.

The interview process should ideally be a conversation in which you are the most interesting person in the world. It won't be a back-and-forth sharing session. It's all about you; about what you do, what you think and how this or that happened in your life. That's the whole point of the interview process.

I suggest going chapter by chapter after having establishing your word count. Let's say our architect's book will be around 50,000 words (the average number of words for a business book), and he will have ten chapters, that's roughly 5,000 words per chapter.

To keep it simple, let's say the first chapter is called "My Arizona Childhood" and talks about growing up in Bullhead City, Arizona. That could be a boring chapter. (Come on, be honest!) He might lose his readers before he gets started.

What if the interviewer asks these ten questions, and Brian Tracy gives 1,000-word answers to each?

❏ Was there a single piece of interesting architecture in Bullhead City? If so, what was it?

❏ How old were you when you visited a bigger city and saw your first notable building?

❏ Can you tell me how you felt and what you thought when you first saw that building?

❏ How did your parents shape your future career? Was it because they were professionals or because they were not?

❏ Did you daydream of buildings while sitting in English class?

❏ Bullhead City is very hot. How did living in that intense heat influence what would become your particular design style?

❏ Is Bullhead City a place to run from or to come home to? Tell me about that.

❏ Did those around you when you were a child support your desire to design? How?

❏ If you could step back in time and cross paths with that little person growing up in Bullhead City and give him a critical warning, what would it be?

❑ What specific advice would you tell your younger self?

It takes an average of 7.7 minutes to answer each question when speaking in 1,000 word answers. Multiply 7.7 by 10, and in just over an hour, you've completed a draft of a first chapter.

If you meet your interviewer for one hour per week, in just under three months you will easily be able to complete ten chapters, plus two more interviews for follow-up and clarification talks. It's a simple matter of math. Rinse and repeat, and you will have a book written before you know it!

Where to outsource getting ideas out of your head
Credo
Fiverr
FreeeUp
Freelancer
Hubstaff Talent
Outsourcely
PeoplePerHour
Textbroker
Upwork
Workhoppers

Cost

You could probably get away with $1,500 for the interviewing and transcription of the 50,000-word example book mentioned above, but this doesn't include the actual writing which comes next.

CHAPTER 4

Transcript to Manuscript

At Leaders Press, we have highly skilled interviewers and ghostwriters who take care of the book-creation process. For the sake of simplicity, however, let's assume that your ghostwriter is the person interviewing you to get the ideas out of your head. (If you are doing your own recording, you will probably be outsourcing your material as well.)

At the conclusion of each interview, you will have an audio file that will need to be transcribed. While some writers will do transcriptions, most do not. Like any other part of the book-writing process, most writers — you guessed it — outsource.

Why?

I'm sure you've heard that old saying about remaining true to the *highest and best* use of your time. You've realized by now that while you have a story, advice, history, dos and don'ts, information or some variety of how-to you want to share, the *highest and best* use of your time is to impart that information to others. It's not to type it, organize it, edit it, format it, design the cover, and market it.

(You've seen those reviews on self-published books on Amazon that read, "I wish the writer would have hired an editor!", "Too many typos!", "I couldn't finish reading because there were so many mistakes and spelling errors!", haven't you?)

Shudder.

While your job is to impart information to your interviewer, other professionals have similar decisions to make. Each step of the writing process has a specialist. Up to this point, we have discussed the writer/interviewer, and now the transcriptionist. (In later chapters, we will talk about the editors, formatters, cover designers and marketers.)

Let's return to our architect, Brian Tracy. Would he build a structure with his own hands? Would he order the supplies? Would he bog himself down by evaluating pricing comparisons for materials? Would he also act as the lighting designer, the landscape designer, the interior designer and the landlord? (You already know the answers to those questions!) Brian Tracy will not do any such thing; he will outsource each task. He remains true to the highest and best use of his time, which is to design buildings. Similarly, once the audio file of each of your interviews is complete, it will need to be transcribed by a professional. If your ghostwriter is handling the transcription process, you're golden. If you are doing your interviews and having them transcribed, where do you find transcriptionists?

I use Rev, and I highly recommend them. They offer a 24-hour turnaround at the cost of $1 per minute. I hope you don't think, "Wow! A dollar a minute really adds up." Well, it does. The alternatives, however, such as hiring cheap labor or spending hours and hours doing it yourself, are unpleasant.

The transcription piece is essential. If it's a failure, your ghostwriter will be looking at errors that he or she may not catch. (After all, your subject specialty isn't necessarily clear to them.) Moreover, if the transcription isn't completed in a timely fashion, your schedule can get bogged down in a hurry.

You can try your luck on Upwork or other outsourcing sites mentioned throughout this book to find transcriptionists as well. (I warn you, though, this takes even more of your valuable time, and that is time spent doing things not of your *highest and best* use.)

Once you've chosen a transcriptionist, your ghostwriter can work with it, and it will be time for the actual writing!

Where to outsource transcript to manuscript

Rev — for transcription

Credo

Fiverr

FreeeUp

Freelancer

Hubstaff Talent

Outsourcely

PeoplePerHour

Textbroker

Upwork

Workhoppers

Cost

The average cost for transcription is $1 per minute. I've found the math to approximate a 1:3 structure, meaning for every hour of speaking, there will be three hours of transcribing.

When you shop around online, you'll find that depending on the source, quality and book length, the fees for ghostwriting generally range between $18,000 and $150,000+. It's possible to find lower-priced offers but bear in mind that the range in talent varies as much as the range in prices! (That's strictly writing, which doesn't include any of the upcoming steps, such as editing, cover design, marketing or launch.)

CHAPTER 5

Developmental Editing

At this point, you should have the first draft of your manuscript — but hold on! I know you're excited, but you're not ready to publish it just yet.

First, double check to see if you've followed the 25-50-75 percent framework mentioned in Step 2 to identify any missing elements.

As a reminder, here it is again:

- ❑ a 'hook' that is so fascinating that the readers continue to read on;
- ❑ a 25 percent point of no return;
- ❑ a 50 percent midpoint;
- ❑ a 75 percent point;
- ❑ a satisfying ending (and a call to action).

I already know your book is impressive. You and your ghostwriter have done a phenomenal job of working together by combining your knowledge and their writing skills to craft your bestseller.

But — and this is a big but — your book must go thorough several rounds of editing. If you don't take this step, don't even think of hitting publish and putting your book on the market. The readers could chew you up in their reviews, and you don't want that to happen.

Let's take a quick look at three types of editors:

- ❑ developmental editor;
- ❑ copy editor;
- ❑ proofreader.

(Do you need to hire a specific editor for each step? That's a great question, and I will answer it in just a moment.)

The developmental editor reviews a manuscript for plot flow. She tightens and sharpens your prose and provides a chapter-by-chapter analysis. This type of editor gives you a helicopter view of what needs to be improved in your manuscript by concentrating on the overall picture and concept.

The copy editor does the line-by-line editing. At this step, she checks for punctuation, spelling errors, word usage, capitalization and grammar. Your manuscript is reviewed for duplication of words and phrases. The editor reviews for the use of adverbs, consistency, ambiguity, incorrect statements and logic. She also reviews for mechanics, paragraph construction and dialogue.

Finally, we have the proofreader, who goes through your final product to make sure everything is as perfect as possible. Often your copy editor will take care of the proofreading as well.

(It might be tempting to skip the editors and use an online service such as Grammarly. Grammarly is terrific, but — and this is a big but — it will not be able to do the type of editing I've described above.)

To circle back around to the question of whether you need to hire a different person for each editing step, very often you can work with one person who can do each type of editing. She can do the helicopter view editing while acting as the developmental editor. Then she can go through your book line-by-line and address specific concerns. Finally, she can proofread your book once you've fixed any developmental issues and catch every typo. (And yes, there will be developmental concerns and typos!)

Instead of having to hire a developmental editor up-front, you could address developmental editing or developmental troubleshooting in a critique group. It's possible to find beta readers who can catch any problems and typos. Encourage them to speak up if they find any issues or problems with the manuscript! If you join a critique group and use beta readers, they will catch your developmental issues, and then you can hire a copy editor/proofreader to polish your manuscript. While working with critique groups and beta readers is a low-cost (or no-cost) alternative, I highly recommend that you hire a developmental editor to go over your book.

In a later chapter, we will talk about getting early reviews for your book and how to find those reviewers before you launch. We'll mention this later as you'll need to encourage them to share what they think. If the manuscript needs more work, it goes back to the ghostwriter again. Otherwise, it's time to move on to copy editing.

Where to outsource developmental editing

Editorial Freelancers Associations

Fiverr

Independent Editors Group

Kibin

Kirkus Editorial

Postscripting

Preditors & Editors

Readers' Favorite

Scribendi

Upwork

Cost

Editing tends to average around $.08 per word, so for a 50,000-word book it would amount to $4,000.

CHAPTER 6

Copy Editing

Copy editors will ensure every comma, semicolon and period is in the correct place. Their specialty is grammar and spelling, and although it can be a tedious portion of your editing process, it pays off in the end when you don't have to deal with negative reviews criticizing the quality of your work.

I advise that if you can, find one person who can do it all. The process will be much more seamless in working with one editor. I recommend that you develop a good relationship and stick with her, especially if you're doing a series of books. It's a good idea to work with the same person, as it provides for continuity of text. Sometimes, however, you might first need to hire a couple of editors (or even more) to see who is the best fit for you and who does the type of work that you expect to be done.

Where do you find a good editor?

Here are some examples of where to find these essential specialists:

- ❑ Editorial Freelancers Associations;
- ❑ Fiverr;
- ❑ Independent Editors Group;
- ❑ Kibin;
- ❑ Kirkus Editorial;

- ☐ Postscripting;
- ☐ Preditors & Editors;
- ☐ Readers' Favorite;
- ☐ Scribendi;
- ☐ Upwork.

If you go to our good friend Fiverr or Upwork and type in copy editing, you'll find many people who do copy editing. Of course, just like with ghostwriters, you can give them a sample to test their skills. If you like their work, you can discuss exactly what you want them to do, hire them, and try them out. Another website that is dedicated explicitly to editors is called Preditors and Editors. Browse through the site and see if anyone catches your eye. They also provide other services, such as ghostwriting, and they help you avoid phishing scams on the Internet. You can also check out Independent Editors Group, where they do manuscript evaluations, developmental editing, line editing and proofreading. Then there's Kirkus Editorial — you can get a free quote up-front. Editorial Freelancers Association is another winner, and you can also check them out to look for editing services. Readers' Favorite is one of my preferred options, as I'm the founder and moderator of the Readers' Favorite Forum, so I'm probably biased. But I have used their services, and they did one round of proofreading for me. You can check them out and see if they meet your requirements.

Of course, there's nothing like word of mouth. If you use an editor and you're happy with him, and he's looking for more work, please share his contact information with others. It's always best when we can share professionals whom we've already worked with, and we're happy enough to recommend them to others. I work with trusted professionals for all of my editing. One of them is my former English teacher. He's edited plenty of books for me and has the skills to finds developmental inconsistencies, as well as take the book through comprehensive rounds of copy editing and proofreading.

To recap, there are three types of editing you will need: developmental editing, copy editing and proofreading. Don't skip any of the editing steps! Each step is crucial!

How can you successfully market a bestseller if readers leave reviews such as "This book was full of typos!"? (If it is indeed full of typos, they will leave those reviews, I promise!) Don't risk it! There are certain things you must address before your customers see the finished product. Outsourcing for writers and editors will help to produce the best product possible. Otherwise, you'll be wasting your time marketing a product that is only a lukewarm hit. You don't want a book like that; you want the best book you can produce at the moment!

How much will editing cost? Here are some prices that you might be looking at, and naturally, they vary widely. You could be looking at $30-60 per hour depending on what you hire your editor to do. Some charge per word.

Where to outsource copy editing

Editorial Freelancers Associations

Fiverr

Independent Editors Group

Kibin

Kirkus Editorial

Postscripting

Preditors & Editors

Readers' Favorite

Scribendi

Upwork

Cost

At around $.018 per word, it would amount to $900 for a 50,000-word book.

CHAPTER 7

Interior Layout and Formatting

As you work with transcriptionists, ghostwriters and editors, you'll probably use a Microsoft Word document. That format works for internal communication, but it will need to be converted to other formats for publishing. Sites, such as Amazon, will provide a list of file types acceptable for publishing; they include ePub, MOBI and PDF files.

This can be a challenge because it's technical and often outside an author's area of expertise. Guess what — I recommend outsourcing to get this done professionally, or you'll risk the chance of receiving negative reviews based on formatting.

Will you need an e-book?

The answer is an unequivocal "Yes". The number of readers choosing e books is continually growing as the number of devices purchased grows. Specific winning pricing strategies can only be achieved with e-books, and we'll talk more about those later.

To understand why you need an e-book, you need to know how people read. Many people use an e-reader, such as Kindle, and some people read books on their computers. People read on their tablets, such as an iPad, and some people read on their cell phones.

As a writer, you need to satisfy all those readers. If you don't provide the format they're seeking, you're leaving money on the table.

So what's the digital format?

The primary digital format is called an ePub, and that's what you'll need to convert your Word, Pages or Scrivener document into for the platform called Kindle Direct Publishing (KDP), which is where you'll publish your Kindle books on Amazon. KDP uses MOBI, which is another digital format, but it can convert it perfectly from an ePub.

There are different approaches you can use to convert your books to a digital format. You can do it yourself, as the cheap and easy approach, or you can outsource.

You will likely receive a Word file of your book from your ghostwriter. The cheap and easy approach is to get an ePub from your KDP dashboard. When you set up your book, Point 7 is to preview your book. Once you've uploaded your book in Word format, you can preview it. If you click the 'preview book' button at the bottom, it says 'downloadable previewer'. The orange, underlined sentence is where you download the book preview file. When you download that, you have your ePub which you can then use to submit to other publishers. Many other platforms accept Word. So if you work in Microsoft Word, and you have a novel or nonfiction with no or few images, you can upload that directly to your dashboard. That's a very easy approach that requires no additional cost or skills.

Next, for Mac users, there is Pages, which is the Mac equivalent of Word. With Pages, you can go to the file and export directly to ePub.

For children's books, you can use the Kindle Kids' Book Creator, which is for Kindle books only. You can also use iBooks author, which is for Apple iBooks only. The downside with both the Kindle Kids' Book Creator and iBooks Author is that they can only be used for their respective platforms. You can only use the Kids' Book Creator to create books for Kindle so it won't work on other platforms. You can't upload to iBooks, for example, because this creates your book in the MOBI file for Amazon.

That's the least expensive (and most time consuming) approach. Now let's look at the do-it-yourself professional approach.

If you haven't heard of Scrivener, you need to have it, unless you're a children's author. If you write anything apart from children's books, Scrivener is the best software ever. It's fantastic for writing, and I used to write my books in Scrivener before outsourcing the formatting and layout. Even though there's a learning curve when you start using it, it's fantastic for converting because it converts in all possible formats. In Scrivener, there's a compile function. Then you customize how you want your book to look, and you have a choice of formats. You can convert it to Word, OpenOffice, PDF, ePub, etc. The one-time cost is $45, and it's worth it.

Then there's Vellum, which is software for Mac, and their tagline is that they create beautiful books. It's convenient that while you're writing, you can see precisely how your reader will view it. It's the more expensive option, and it's only for Mac users. There's a one time cost of $199, and they also have a per-book plan.

There are others including Sigil, which is free. The free software is advertised as being for anyone, but there's some learning curve involved. If you're going to spend some time to learn new software, that software should be something that you can also use to write your book, so I would go for Scrivener.

Then there's Jutoh, which is either $39 or $80, depending on the option you choose.

Free sites include Calibre and LibreOffice.

If you like to outsource completely, I recommend AtRiteX.

To sum up, here's what you can use:

- ❑ Adobe Indesign (excellent for children's books, learning curve, various payment plans)
- ❑ AtRiteX
- ❑ Calibre (free)
- ❑ Jutoh ($39; $80 for Jutoh Plus)
- ❑ LibreOffice (free)
- ❑ Scrivener ($45)
- ❑ Sigil (free)
- ❑ Vellum ($199 or pay per title $29)

Okay, so you understand that people read on Kindles, other e-readers, computers, tablets and cell phones. Do you also need a paperback with e-books on the rise? The answer is "Yes".

Why?

Even though e-readers are on the rise, many, if not most, readers still like paperback books. If they love a particular e-book, they will often want the book in paperback form as well.

It would help if you had a paperback to get into bookstores and libraries, to do book signings and book fairs, and to hold your book at award ceremonies. There's also nothing like holding something you wrote in your own hands.

Now let's look at the types of printing. There's POD — or print on demand — and the two companies that are, for now, the only players are KDP Print (which used to be CreateSpace) and IngramSpark. With POD, there's no initial investment, but there's a higher cost per unit. It's integrated with Amazon in KDP Print, and with the library system in the case of IngramSpark, so distribution is covered. There's no inventory for you, and it's an excellent solution for online sales. Amazon is the key player.

With Amazon, there's no setup cost. They only create paperbacks at this time, so no hardbacks yet. If you want to change your manuscript and upload a new one, there's no fee, so you can do it an infinite number of times.

IngramSpark is an entirely different animal. There is a setup cost for every book and format. Currently, the price is $49 for each title you want to create. If you're going to create an e-book, paperback or a hardback you pay a setup fee for each. Once you upload your book in IngramSpark and you want to change something, you need to pay again. It's not as easy to use as Amazon. It's not integrated with Amazon, so it doesn't cover the Amazon territory.

In theory, Amazon has expanded distribution as it has an option that libraries could request your books. In reality, libraries are less incentivized to buy from them as they are the middleman (which is more expensive) and they don't offer returns.

With IngramSpark, if the library wants to return a book, you can select whether you want that book physically back or whether you want them to destroy it. Whatever selection you make, those returns are available, and that's crucial for a library to get your book.

In choosing between Amazon or IngramSpark, I recommend that you publish with Amazon and then later with IngramSpark for libraries. When you are at the point that your book is perfect and you won't change anything — not the cover or anything in the text — only then is it time to get your book in IngramSpark because they charge you for every change you make.

At Leaders Press, we not only work with Amazon's KDP Print and IngramSpark, but we also have a partnership with Ingram Publisher Services for sales and distribution. Ingram Publisher Services is the world's most extensive and most reliable distribution network, combined with a sales team of passionate book lovers and access to the industry's leading e-book and POD technologies. Thanks to Ingram, we have a dedicated sales team plus 100 market reps that connect us to wherever books are sold. We also have access to state-of-the-art warehousing and distribution.

Since not everyone can have such a partnership with Ingram, let's focus on working around it by looking at offset printing. There's a substantial initial investment in offset printing because you have to pay for every book printed before they're sold, but the cost per book is lower. This will not, however, be integrated with Amazon or the library system, so you do have to take care of your distribution, and you'll need an inventory.

When you order books this way, you'll have an inventory of 1,000, 2,000 or 5,000 books, so you'll have to keep them somewhere. Some of my author friends have their garages filled with books. Others have half of their living room full of books, so figure out how you will store your inventory if you choose this option. Usually, you pay for inventory unless you have room to store massive amounts of books in your house or garage. This is, however, an excellent solution for bulk orders and we will talk more about these later, but if you get any bulk orders, offset is the way to go.

The next question is where to print. The two main players are China and the United States. In China, there is a lower cost per unit than in the U.S. There's nowhere else where you will get a lower cost for printing a book than in China at the moment. There will, however, be a minimum order of 1,000, or in some places, 2,000. They won't even talk about printing books if you don't order at least 2,000 copies. Then you must add the shipping cost, which will make the overall price still more economical than if you print in the US. Add customs fees, which according to some sources could amount to 60 percent per book. It is, however, a long execution time. It usually takes months before they create your book, and send you the digital proof, and then many more additional months before you get the book in your hands.

In the U.S., there is a higher cost per unit than in China, but a lower shipping cost. If you live in the U.S., it costs less — no customs if you live in the US, and you will experience a faster execution.

Here's more detail on printers in China.

- ❑ A.F. Offset Printing Company

    They print all kinds of books, gift boxes and packages.

- ❑ East Color Printing Packaging Company

    This is a manufacturer of children's books with 10 years' experience.

- ❑ Guangzhou Xin Yi Printing Company

    It prints softcover and hardcover books, and children's books, including board books.

- ❑ Hangzhou Lihe Digital Technology Company

    This is a professional manufacturer, devoted to providing global clients with book printing, package producing and film printing services. They offer high-quality custom children's books.

- ❑ Hunan Yongzhou Benteng Color Printing Company

    It specializes in print books and magazines.

- ❑ Ming Hong Ming He Paper Products

    It specializes in children's books including board books, pop-up books, sticker books, puzzles.

- ❑ Zhejiang Jiayi Color Printing Company

    It specializes in printing children's books, including board books, pop-up books and jigsaw books.

❑ Zhejiang Sino-Light Mediatek Company

> It specializes in children's books, including board books, pop-up books, puzzle books, activity books, EVA books and sounds books.

Here are details of major printers in the U.S.

❑ Color House Graphics

> This is a book manufacturer dedicated to providing top-notch services to authors and publishers around the country.

❑ King Printing

> This is a short-run book printing company and book manufacturer. It specializes in short-run printing and binding for self-published authors, individuals, small businesses and book publishers.

MCRL Overseas Printing is a combination of the two main options. It offers production in China with the ease and standards of the Canadian business environment. It offers complete printing and production management solutions. It's a hybrid printing option recommended to us by several award-winning authors.

To recap, you will need formats, including ePub, MOBI and PDF. For paperback or hardback, you have two options. The first is print on demand (POD), which is either Amazon or IngramSpark, and the second is printing in bulk with offset.

Where to outsource layout and formatting

AtRiteX

Cost

for simple text, probably around $200

CHAPTER 8

An Attention-Grabbing Cover

You should know by now that a book has to *fit in*. A big part of a lucrative genre is where there's already demand, so it must *fit in* and *stand out*. It has to have its unique selling proposition. The cover, similarly, has to *fit in* and especially, it has to *fit in* to the bestselling covers in your genre.

You know that old saying about how you can't judge a book by its cover? Cliché maybe, but in the world of online publishing, it's definitely false. Here's a cover fact: readers do judge a book by its cover. Bearing that in mind, you need to create the type of cover that will draw the readers' attention. Work to make your cover visually appealing by focusing on two main elements: title and artwork.

Why do readers buy a book?

Readers buy a book when it's recommended by a friend, written by their favorite author, or it caught their eye while browsing. The third reason is crucial for you. When you look at bestselling books in your category, you want your book's cover to look like it was made in the same place, like it came from the same basket. You don't want readers to see all the books, and then yours as something different from the high standard. They might think, "Oh, this one is self-published for sure." You don't want people to be able to tell.

Your book must *stand out*, as you don't want to copy another author's cover or emulate it too closely. You want it to look like it came from the same place, but yet have a unique touch.

It makes a lot of sense to hire a professional for your cover, even if it hurts your wallet a bit. For the book cover, you want a book-cover designer — not a person who can sculpt or do beautiful paintings — because a designer needs to deal with fonts and balance, and have an understanding of how it will look as a thumbnail on Amazon. When creating artwork, be mindful that Amazon and other retailers and search engines often only show a thumbnail of your cover. That's why it needs to *stand out*. The title should take up at least one third of the cover, nowadays even two thirds, so that it's clearly visible in the thumbnail.

Your cover needs to have large font and be easy to read since it's viewed as a thumbnail. For the same reason, it needs one large image so you can see it well when you look at the thumbnail version. Possibly, it needs to be high contrast, as it attracts the browser's attention. When you have a dark background and a bright element emerging from it, for example, that catches the reader's eye.

Of course, I recommend that you outsource the cover design to a book-cover designer. First, I suggest that you check out the bestselling book covers in your genre. Then ask your cover designer to emulate the covers that have a large image, big font and high contrast going on.

Here are some cover no-nos:

- ❑ no Comic Sans or Papyrus as a font unless it's a humorous book;
- ❑ no use of all the colors of the rainbow or each letter in a different color;
- ❑ no more than two fonts or special styling;

- ☐ no underlining;
- ☐ no weird stuff;
- ☐ no amateurish artwork;
- ☐ no cheap clip art;
- ☐ no pictures that you've drawn yourself unless you're a professional;
- ☐ no children's artwork;
- ☐ no images placed inside a box.

Finally...

- ☐ Don't design your cover yourself.

You have to stay simple. Otherwise, the book cover will look like a crowded joke. You want a professional looking cover to convey your professionalism as an author and using cheap clip art will make readers think the content of your book is cheap as well. You don't want to use one of those standard templates and have your book cover look like all the other amateurish book covers. Your book cover must reflect what you've written. Your cover should tell the reader that you are the best of the best!

Let's take a look at a few different ways you can get your cover professionally designed. At the end of this chapter, I list some sites you can visit, but I'll briefly discuss a few of them.

There is Damonza, and their prices generally range from $500 to $800. You will get a high-quality cover, but there are other ways that you can get a high-quality cover.

Extended Imagery is the service that Jay Conrad — one of the bestselling self-published authors — uses. One of their predesigned covers sells for $200, but I would advise against that as you could have the same cover as another author and pay $200 for the privilege.

Let's take a look at other places where you can have a fantastic cover designed for much less.

One of my favorites is 99 Designs. Check them out, but you will likely spend $300 to more than $1,000. They do have a rather interesting execution because there'll be a selection of 30 to 90 designs to choose from! You'll be able to pick the best design from some top designers, but you'll spend a lot of money to do it. You will get many designs as people compete for your design. The exciting thing is that they will make a few designs and they will all be different. The trick is to give a high rating to the ones that you do like, because when you give them five stars, you get more designers creating similar covers to the ones that you like and then you get to choose the finalists.

You can also use Fiverr, as there are many gigs on Fiverr starting at $5! Find an artist on Fiverr, check out their artwork, and ask them to create a simple book cover. (It won't have bells and whistles if it is just the $5 version.) Send them the covers you like and specify that you want a large image, large fonts and high contrast. You should get back something similar. If not, you can revise it. You tell them if you don't want the color they've chosen, or you want the font to be a little bigger, or the image to be a bit more transparent, or have more contrast. I recommend that you always order just the e-book first because you won't know if you will like the front cover. If you like the front cover, you can upgrade. You might hit the jackpot and get a great cover for $20. In several instances, Fiverr artists created amazing covers for my books. In some cases, the covers were only so-so. It's a little bit hit and miss, but with that price, you can't expect to have a hit every time. You can test by ordering more than one cover. It's a good idea to ask two different cover artists to create a book cover for $5 each, and then you can test those covers.

How do you test a cover?

Email your list or your friends. Do a poll on Facebook if you're part of a Facebook group for authors (I include a full list of the best Facebook groups for authors in my award-winning guide *How I Sold 80,000 Books*). There are several groups for authors where you can ask for feedback on your covers. We'll talk about it in the promotion section. Alternatively, do a poll on your private Facebook page.

To recap, your cover should be professionally designed. Whether you spend $5 or $1,000 on your cover, that's up to you. You may get a great $5 cover and you might get a $1,000 dud if you don't know which types of covers sell and can't judge your designer's capabilities.

Either way, your cover should look like a bestselling cover. We discussed the elements such as large image, large font and high contrast. Make sure your cover looks great as a thumbnail. Readers will judge your book by its cover. Make sure it makes an excellent first impression.

Where to outsource a cover

Damonza

Fiverr

99designs

Cost

between $5 and $1,000

CHAPTER 9

Optimization for Online Sales

Amazon may look like a digital bookstore, but it's really a search engine. That's why it's vital to optimize your book for online sales. Think about what readers will search for, and optimize your title and subtitle with keywords to get your book at the top of their search results. Software, such as KDP Rocket, can help you determine the best keywords.

Another aspect of optimization is choosing the right category, so your book will be visible to readers who are searching for books about that topic. Let's start by looking at some facts. The category you choose has a direct impact on your bestseller status as you can only choose two categories. (A secret I can share is that there are hidden categories that can increase your possibility of achieving bestseller status!)

What is it like to be a bestselling author?

As a *USA Today*, *Wall Street Journal* and Amazon bestselling author, I can assure you that it's a phenomenal feeling. Achieving this status also greatly increases your authority as people pay more attention to a bestselling author than to a regular author. While landing on the *USA Today* and *Wall Street Journal* bestseller lists is very rewarding, it's also extremely difficult to achieve (more about this later). It's much easier to become an Amazon bestselling author when you know what you're doing. I have the positioning and launch so dialed in that I guarantee all our Leaders Press authors that they will hit No. 1 in their category and become Amazon bestselling authors.

I don't have to explain why that's attractive. You can call yourself a bestselling author and you can use this badge everywhere — on your website, on your social media, on your business cards, on your catalogs, in your email signature. It's worth taking time to understand how to place your book in the correct categories to achieve bestseller status. Amazon ultimately wants to sell more books, so it will promote strong sellers. If you can help Amazon, they will make more money, and they will help you make more money.

How do you select the best categories?

Take the No. 1 book in a category where you think your book *fits in*, and see what its overall Amazon ranking is. Let's say it's 2,900, which is an excellent ranking. That means that this book is the 2,900[th] most sold on Amazon out of millions of books available. It'll be hard to beat this book; it'll be hard to get to No. 1 in this category and to 2,900 in the Kindle store. It's pretty hard to get there, but it's easier to beat this book than a book that's No. 50 in the paid Kindle store.

Now you look for a different category with a lower ranking. Continue doing that until you find a category in which book No. 1 has the lowest possible ranking. Do that to figure out the best two categories for your book. So you want a category where it's easy to be No. 1 but you also want a category that sells, so look at the 100th book in that category and make sure that it has a ranking below 100,000. If it's a ranking in the millions, it means that that category isn't very lucrative and you probably shouldn't have written a book on that subject to begin with.

Now I want to show you a little trick, which is to find the hidden categories. There's a book called *Nobody Wants to Read*

Your Sh*t: Why That Is And What You Can Do About It. At the moment, this book is at 19,000 as a top Amazon e-book seller, and it's No. 13 in Creativity. Yet there is something exciting. While it's No. 13 in Creativity, it's No. 11 in Authorship.

How is that and why didn't we see Authorship before?

Because it's a hidden category. Now let's say you want your book to be in the Authorship category. If you can be No. 11 in Authorship, that's better than No. 13 in Creativity, correct?

How do you get into a hidden category?

When you publish, you'll be asked to select the two categories your book best fits. You will choose No. 1 as we discussed for this example, which is creativity. For the second category, you won't be able to find Authorship because it's hidden, so you'll choose the option 'unclassifiable'. Next, you write to KDP support and say, "My book's second category is unclassifiable. Can you please place my book in Authorship in the Kindle store? This is how my book should be classified." Of course, they can say that they decide where your book should be, but I've never had a problem with them granting my request.

Hidden categories will not be available to select in your KDP dashboard, so you choose unclassifiable as one of the categories. When you contact KDP support to ask them to place your book in the hidden category, you will copy and paste that exact whole string from the beginning to the end. For example, you would not just ask for Authorship but for the full string:

Kindle Store > Kindle e-books > Reference > Writing, Research & Publishing Guides > Publishing & Books > Authorship.

If you wrote a book about fasting, you could find hidden categories that include Diet Therapy, Naturopathy and Psychoneuroimmunology. The string that you would include in your request to KDP support would look like this:

Kindle Store > Kindle e-books > Medical e-books > Alternative & Holistic > Diet Therapy

Kindle Store > Kindle e-books > Health, Fitness & Dieting > Alternative Medicine > Naturopathy

Kindle Store > Kindle e-books > Medical e-books > Alternative & Holistic > Mind-Body Medicine (Psychoneuroimmunology).

Choose your categories wisely so that you can become a No. 1 bestselling author quite easily. You're going to have to do some searching on Amazon to find the best hidden categories for your book, but do it because it's worth it. You might think this is a case of being a big fish in a relatively small pond. It's no different, however, from having the best organic Cantonese restaurant in your city. If you're the best in your specific category, it will definitely attract interest.

To recap, search for books that are similar to yours, find the category in which you have the highest probability of becoming a bestselling author, select unclassified on your KDP dashboard, and write to KDP to request that your book be placed in that category by copying and pasting the entire string. Spend some time searching for the best ones because this can make or break your No. 1 Amazon bestselling status. It's worth doing the homework.

Now here's another secret few authors know. Even though you officially only get two categories, if you can manually find more categories that your book belongs to, you can let Amazon know, and they will give you up to ten categories for your book to rank in!

Next, we'll talk about keywords alchemy. Keywords are the words you'll use to describe your book succinctly, and alchemy will be the combination of your keywords. There is a magic science to this! Dave Chesson is the creator of KDP Rocket, which is fantastic software to use to determine your keywords. I was fortunate enough to work with him on keywords, so the next portion of the book will include his advice. Before we jump in, I want to mention the two times when we should do keyword research. Most authors will do keyword research right when they're ready to publish or when they're changing up keywords to introduce their book to new markets. That's an excellent tactic that I will drill down into. The most critical time to do keyword research, however, is before you start writing your book.

Keyword research in truth is a way to figure out if there is an existing market on Amazon that is actively searching for what you plan to write. This research will immediately tell you whether or not you can depend on Amazon to make sales for you. Your keyword research may tell you that nobody on Amazon is searching for your keywords. If that happens, it doesn't mean you can't write the book, but it does mean that you can't depend on Amazon to send people to your book. You'll have to find the market somewhere else on the Internet and bring them to your sales page on Amazon. Sometimes you'll learn that your market doesn't exist yet. That's okay. You need to know that you will have that extra step of finding your market and bringing them to you.

So what does KDP Rocket do?

It immediately identifies which markets do and don't already exist on Amazon. On your KDP Rocket dashboard, you type in keywords and the software will show you where the demand exists on Amazon, if they're using a particular word, if they're searching for your type of product, and what they're paying for the product. As you play around with the word combinations, you will know exactly what you need to target. Those words become your list of keywords.

To step back for a moment, there are two ways to market your book — write the book for an existing market or go out and find the market and bring them to your book. By doing your research before you write the book, you'll know which way to go. Hopefully, you get to do both, because that builds your sales. I want to mention that nonfiction and fiction readers are very different in their keyword styles due to their psychologies being completely different. With nonfiction, readers tend to search for the pain point such as what you want to leave, relieve, do or not do (that applies to self-help books but also to biography, history and science books in which the author is addressing a particular question or problem). Fiction is entirely different. There is no how-to, and no pain point. It's strictly about entertainment. Whatever the case, as long as people are going to Amazon and typing something into the search box, keywords will be a part of the whole book-marketing process.

Here are some tactics which will be applicable for anyone seeking to optimize for online sales. Let's say you want to write a book about horses, specifically horse books for women. Keywords for this category weren't hot in a demographic search. I niched down on types of horses. I pulled up a Googled list of horse breeds. Perhaps there was one particular type of horse that people are jazzed about and there are opportunities inside of that? I didn't find too much there. I soon learned that the hot market was around how to raise horses; the how-to type of books. I saw that one of the things that potentially could be an opportunity from the beginning was to add a spiritual element to the book, such as how working with horses can help people with their spirituality. I know there's a market on how to raise horses, so I thought of the potential to create a book on how to raise horses, but have an underlying message that in raising horses, you can lift yourself spiritually as well.

One of the great things for new authors who don't have a large following or email list is that writing for an existing market allows you to get in front of new people. With a 100,000-person email list and a giant blog, you can send people to your books. Otherwise, you've got to be pretty smart about your keywords. Identifying a target market and knowing which words people are using when searching for that book on Amazon will give you that opportunity to make sure that your book is right there in front of the right people.

Sometimes we uncover a hidden keyword for a published book, and it can be a game changer. Those things happen, but they're not the magic bullet. By setting up a game plan before you start writing and knowing your market, and which words readers are using, and by using keywords to create your title and subtitle, you'll have much greater success. Using that market data, you'll have a stronger foothold and a good start right from the beginning. As writers, we're artists, and we'll always have a story that we want to write; however, without being able to grab a market from somewhere else and bring people to your book, you have to know the crowd in the room so you can deliver the right message.

Where to outsource optimizing your book for online sales

Many of my co-authors of *Write and Grow Rich* have solid knowledge on this.

Cost

It should be possible to optimize your book for online sales during a 60-minute coaching call. That costs about $600.

CHAPTER 10

A Captivating Book Description

One thing I commonly see is when authors write a valuable 50,000-word book but then write a lackluster book description that doesn't convince the reader to buy the book. Writing a compelling book description is fundamentally good copywriting. You use copywriting all the time, whether you write books, book descriptions or emails. As an author, you should master the skill of copywriting.

The absolute guru of copywriting is Gary Halbert. He passed away, but his sons run his website www.thegaryhalbertletter.com. He used to charge for these letters that he would send by direct mail to people, and it was costly to receive them. When I was studying copywriting, I would click on those letters and copy them, retyping them on my computer to fix his writing patterns in my mind. Today, I still use his great letter about AIDA (attention, interest, desire, action) to write all my descriptions, and do other types of copywriting.

For example, here's the description I created for my book *How I Sold 80,000* Books following the AIDA principle:

- ❑ attention: "Discover how you too can sell 80,000 books even if you haven't sold a single copy yet!"

- ❑ interest: "Warning: Reading this 2016 Readers' Favorite Book Award winner and implementing its strategies may cause a significant income increase."

- ❑ desire: "Get your copy now and discover [compelling bullet points here]."

❏ action: "Scroll up to grab your copy now!"

I recommend that you devote some time to read Gary Halbert's AIDA letter.

You know what the hardest part of writing a sales message is?

It's getting started.

Do you know what is most often the missing ingredient in a sales message?

The sales message doesn't tell an interesting story. That's why I recommend AIDA (attention, interest, desire, action).

Let's take a look at a book description I wrote for a client, Mark Nureddine's *Pocket Mentor*:

> Are you an entrepreneur missing a mentor?
> If so, *Pocket Mentor* is what you've been looking for.
>
> Not only do you get a comprehensive guide to launching and building a lasting business, but you also get complimentary access to the author's exclusive mastermind for entrepreneurs!
>
> Start reading now to:
>
> ❏ discover if you've got what it takes to take your business to 25 years and counting;
> ❏ find out which mistakes you can avoid and how to bounce back if you trip;
> ❏ learn if your business a has the wings to fly figure out your profit margins with a proven formula;
> ❏ discover the type of market research that matters;

- ❑ learn about the legal issues of creating and running a business;

- ❑ find out how to manage your financials;

- ❑ discover proven and new ways to hire;

- ❑ learn how to work effectively with suppliers;

- ❑ understand how to launch your product;

and much more!

Pocket Mentor is the missing link between where you are now and where you want to be. Grab your copy now to take your business idea to the next level!

Following AIDA, how do you grab somebody's attention?

The answer is that it has to be all about the reader. In the first sentence of the book description for *Pocket Mentor*, I ask, "Are you an entrepreneur missing a mentor?" I'm talking directly to the reader, and I immediately get his attention. If he's an entrepreneur, missing a mentor, or just plain curious about the process, I have his attention. Next, I say, "If so, *Pocket Mentor* is what you've been looking for." My first sentence captures his attention, and leads him directly to the second sentence. In other words, he keeps reading — that's always the goal in copywriting (or any other writing).

Now that I have his attention, I go after his interest, and I say, "Not only do you get a comprehensive guide to launching and building a lasting business, you also get complimentary access to the author's exclusive mastermind for entrepreneurs." I want him to be interested, so I entice him by letting him know that if he buys the book, he'll get a complimentary mastermind.

Regarding desire, Gary Halbert says, "Once a prospect is interested in what you are talking about, it is time to get his greed glands going and make him really desire the product or service." The way to build desire (and get his greed glands going) is usually done through bullet points. In *Pocket Mentor's* case, I tell the reader to "start reading now to…", then I give him ten solid reasons for reading, and then describe what he'll find in the book, and tell him there's much more.

The last part of AIDA is action. Every single piece of copy that you write has to be a call to action. Otherwise, why bother? You write a book description to entice someone to take action, which in this case, is to buy a book. The action around *Pocket Mentor* is "Here is this book, so grab your copy now to take your business idea to the next level!"

Attention, interest, desire, action.

Similarly, when you write an email to your subscribers, you need to grab their attention, either in the subject line or in the first sentence of the email. The purpose of the first sentence is to get the readers to read the second sentence. For example, "Are you an entrepreneur missing a mentor?" The purpose of this sentence is for them to read the next sentence. The same is true for each sentence. There are various layers of this and more advanced stuff, but this is the basic framework that you can apply to be in the top 1 percent of people writing stuff online.

I recommend a tool that you can find on the Kindlepreneur website for generating Amazon book descriptions. You can play with it by copying and pasting your book description text into the description generator and see what it comes up with. You can change the size of specific text, or put particular sentences in bold. When you've completed your description, the site will generate a code with HTML tags. You will then copy and paste that into your KDP dashboard. This saves so much time.

You might wonder if your description blurb is the same as your elevator pitch. The answer is "No". An elevator pitch comes in handy when you meet a decision maker and you have one minute or less to impress her with your idea. You have to be able to pitch, present, and possibly close a deal in one minute. For an elevator pitch about your book, you could use the AIDA formula (attention, interest, desire, action), and just not elaborate as much.

Book descriptions, however, require a bit more finesse and time.

To recap, I suggest you read the Gary Halbert letters, and type them on your computer. You'll get a fast and amazing education in copywriting!

Where to outsource a captivating book description

CopyChief is a website for business owners and entrepreneurs who want to hire copywriters. You'll be able to find, vet, and hire seasoned copywriters with a proven track record. I first learned about this site from my mentor Dean Jackson at a mastermind. I haven't used it myself because I'm an enthusiastic student of copywriting, and I write my own copy for my books and for clients, but if I were to hire it out, this is the place I'd go to.

Another source is conversionengineering.co where my fellow mastermind member can improve both your book description and any other copy for your business so that you increase your conversions.

Cost

I think you should be able to get it done for $300-$1,000 but this might be a big underestimation. In some cases, copywriters will require a percentage of royalties.

CHAPTER 11

An Outstanding Bio

Now that you have an excellent book with an eye-catching cover and metadata that's optimized for online sales, sell yourself further as an expert by writing an outstanding biographical profile (bio for short).

With your bio, answer the question of why someone should listen to you, or why you're the expert on your topic. The bio is an opportunity to build authority, credibility and likability. As you've no doubt heard many times before, people buy from people they know, like, and trust.

Think of buyers who might be sitting on the fence after searching for keywords, coming across the thumbnail of your book cover, reading your book description... and they're still not convinced. Let's face it, readers have many choices when it comes to buying books. Assume that everyone reads the same how-to books you did, and now every single one of all your competitors has the perfect keywords, the perfect book cover and the perfectly copywritten book description.

What will set you apart at that point?

Your bio!

Be bold and use your bio to get your readers to know, like, and trust you so they will choose your book over your competition. Your bio is a much bigger deal than most authors realize. Think of it as the elevator pitch of your life. (No pressure!) Don't think of it as a resume or a braggadocian mix of sentences. Instead, think of it as the tool that, if done right, will accomplish several things at once:

- drive sales;
- establish your reputation;
- attract media attention;
- establish your credibility or authority.

Let's take a look at the key elements that should be in your bio, while always remembering to say enough, but not too much!

For this exercise, I'm going to use my bio as an example:

> Alinka Rutkowska has sold more than 100,000 books, and she helps others do the same. She is a *USA Today* bestselling author, a *Wall Street Journal* bestselling author and a Top 100 Amazon bestselling author in business and money. Alinka's book-creation process has been showcased in *Entrepreneur* magazine. She's the founder and CEO of Leaders Press, which publishes books by CEOs.

First, whatever your book topic or genre, start by establishing your credentials. Think of this step as very succinctly summarizing why the reader should listen to you. Using my example, the reader should listen to me because I've sold a certain number of books and can help others do the same. Enough said.

Second, include relevant information that builds credibility by talking (briefly!) about your accomplishments. This could include something exciting or unusual — don't be a dud! In my example, I discuss my rankings (because it's very important for what I'm selling). To drive interest, I mention that my book-creation process has been showcased in *Entrepreneur*.

Third, you can mention other books you've written. You will notice that in my bio example, I did not take this step. Why not? Because I'm not capitalizing on what I have written, but what I can help the reader write.

Fourth, name-drop where it counts. You'll notice that I didn't name-drop, but I did mention by name the importance of who ranked my books. I guess you could say that's a subtle form of name-dropping.

Finally, keep your bio short and scintillating. Remember, it's not an autobiography, so you don't need to include the fact that you won that baking contest in fourth grade unless that's your fun fact and you're selling your famous recipes. Every word in your bio should count toward your goal to sell books.

On that note, bios of less than 250 words generally work best. We're quickly becoming a world of sound bites and 140 letters whether you like it not. Stay in the flow and give your readers what they want — a short, concise picture of who you are so they can easily like you.

Where to outsource an outstanding bio

CopyChief

Cost

I think you should be able to get it done for $300-$1,000 but that might be a significant underestimation. In some cases, copywriters will require a percentage of royalties.

CHAPTER 12

Distribution

When your book is ready for distribution, you'll need to consider carefully where and when it will be published. Think about casting a wide net to have the book available via all retailers, or focusing on just one. There are pros and cons to both, and the right decision will depend on your situation and your end goal.

I'm going to cover mainstream online distribution, mainstream offline distribution and undisclosed offline locations. Some of the retailers only accept specific book formats, so we'll also recap some of the things we mentioned in the chapter on layout and formatting. Don't worry, though. It's not as complicated as it may sound.

The book types I cover under online distribution here are both paperbacks and e-books because both of these formats are sold online, but when comparing apples to apples, let's take a look at the US e-book market.

- ❑ No. 1 is Amazon, which holds almost three fourths of the total market share.

- ❑ The second player, holding 11 percent market share, is Apple iBooks.

- ❑ Barnes & Noble's Nook has 8 percent.

- ❑ Kobo has 3 percent.

- ❑ Google Play Books has 2 percent.

- ❑ The remaining retailers make up 2 percent of the market.

With a 74 percent market share, Amazon hardly has any competition. The first thing to do is get your paperbacks and digital books on Amazon. It's the place to go if you decide to print on demand, meaning you won't have any shipping or inventory. When readers go to Amazon's website, they see that your book is always in stock. When they order the book, Amazon takes care of the printing and shipping. You don't need to do anything, so it's a fantastic option if you're not making bulk sales.

If you do offset printing in China, you ship your books to Amazon's warehouse, and they'll take care of the rest. You'll have some handling and shipping to do because Amazon has to have enough stock to be able to cover demand.

The digital version of Amazon for e-books is the Kindle Direct Publishing platform (KDP). KDP is a must. You go through an easy-to-use KDP dashboard. You enter your book details, verify the rights, and target your customers. Then you select your release option, which is either now or a preorder, and you can set your book as available for preorder three months in advance. This is great because then you can build momentum in advance of your book release and get sales which will count towards your sales volume at launch (this is especially valuable if you're aiming at hitting the *USA Today* or *Wall Street Journal* bestseller lists). Then you upload your book and cover, and price it.

Apple iBooks has 11 percent market share, and it's the second largest player after Amazon. To get on iBooks, you have to go via iBooks Author or iTunes Producer. With Apple iBooks Author, it's effortless to drag and drop your book into a beautiful publication. So it's software you download, and then drag and drop your book. The book that you create in iBooks Author unfortunately isn't compatible with any other platform. If you have a lot of images and you're uploading from scratch, it might take a lot of time to create an Apple iBook (which you can't use anywhere else), but it does allow you to create that book for iBooks for free. The alternative is to use Apple iTunes Producer, which you will use to manage your sales and your content. For Apple iTunes Producer, you get your ePub created, and then you upload in that platform. The ePub is suitable for all platforms, so with an ePub, you can use it everywhere.

Next is Barnes & Noble with 8 percent market share. Like Amazon, Barnes & Noble also has its central Barnes & Noble for paperback and a digital platform. Your book will be theoretically available in Barnes & Noble, although not stocked on the shelves. Patrons will be able to request your book. For Barnes & Noble Nook, go to the website and create your book for Nook.

It's a similar process for Kobo and Google Play Books.

Aggregators

An aggregator is a book distributor which distributes your books to numerous retailers. I've just discussed the variety of retailers where you can individually upload your books. An aggregator will do that for you from one website.

Sounds great, right?

Well, there are some pros and cons. A major con is that you get a lower cut if you use an aggregator, as naturally, the aggregator will be paid for doing the work for you. It is, however, easier to do it all in one go, so that's a pro.

I suggest you upload separately to the big retailers we discussed, including Amazon, Apple iBooks, Barnes & Noble, Google Play and Kobo. I recommend you use an aggregator for the rest.

The main aggregators are Draft2Digital, Smashwords and XinXii.

Smashwords is the oldest aggregator. You can upload your documents, and they have what they call a Meatgrinder — software that converts your documents to an ePub. They also accept ePubs but the ePub part is in beta, so there are limitations to it. For example, they won't convert ePubs to other formats, such as MOBI or PDF, so the distribution won't be as broad as if you upload a Word document. Notable retailers in the Smashwords distribution network include Apple, Barnes & Noble, Scribd, Kobo, and Blio. Their library distribution reaches OverDrive, Baker & Taylor Axis 360, Tolino, Gardners, Bibliotheca CloudLibrary, Odilo and Califa's Enki. I've used Smashwords before, and it's especially useful if you write novels or nonfiction with very few pictures. If you write children's picture books, you will upload a fixed-layout ePub, and they have problems distributing that to anywhere else that is not Smashwords. There are limitations for children's books but also for books that you upload as a ready ePub. You should use Smashwords when you're going to upload a Word file. Be warned, though; they have a manual of style that tells you how to prepare your Word document so that the Meatgrinder, which is very sensitive, can convert it to an ePub and other formats.

Draft2Digital (D2D) is a newer aggregator. It has fewer channels right now, so it distributes to the big guys plus

Tolino, OverDrive, Bibliotheca, Scribd, 24Symbols, Playster and Baker & Taylor. D2D accepts .doc, .docx and .epub files for distribution. They have a leaner, user-friendly and more contemporary approach to distributing content. They can also publish your paperback to Amazon, but why publish a paperback through them if you can do it directly via Amazon? If you publish through them, however, they are the publisher, so you won't be able to order author copies for yourself. By publishing directly on Amazon, you can order author copies for yourself, and sell them at a book-signing event. Since it costs you the absolute minimum, you'll have a nice margin. If, however, you publish via D2D, you won't be able to do that; you'll have to pay the full price for your books.

XinXii distributes to major international retailers. It accepts .docx, .epub and .pdf files and some other formats. It distributes to major retailers, including Angus & Robertson in Australia, Livraria Cultura in Brazil, Indigo in Canada, Fnac in France, Thalia (buch.de) in Germany, Mondadori in Italy, Libris in the Netherlands, Whitcoulls in New Zealand, Casa del Libro in Spain, WHSmith in the U.K. and others.

As a recap, upload to the Big 3 (Amazon's KDP, iBooks and Barnes & Noble) on your own. Then use aggregators, such as Smashwords, Draft2Digital and XinXii, to distribute to small retailers. When you set up your book in those aggregators, you can tell them where to distribute your books. You can tell them if you want them to distribute your books to Amazon and iBooks, or you can turn those off and have them distribute only to the smaller retailers.

It can be time-consuming to have to go through Amazon, which is one dashboard, and then iTunes Producer to upload your iBook, then to Barnes & Noble/Nook to upload your book, which are separate dashboards. Then you'd possibly publish with a couple of other big retailers like Kobo and Google Play if you choose, instead of using an aggregator. It is time-consuming, especially if you have an extensive catalog of books, but in the end, you want the most significant possible royalties to come back to you, rather than have them being swallowed by the aggregators. You can choose to do the work up-front, and enjoy the royalties later.

Mainstream offline distribution

The main channels for offline distribution are bookstores and libraries. The prerequisites to get into bookstores and libraries are for your book to be available on IngramSpark or Baker & Taylor's TextStream.

What's the difference between Ingram and Baker & Taylor? Baker & Taylor sells to bookstores as well as to schools and libraries, just as Ingram sells to schools and libraries as well as to bookstores. Each wholesaler, however, has its area of primary strength. IngramSpark is Ingram's service for independent publishers and appears to be much more popular and easy to use than Baker & Taylor's TextStream.

(A quick note about ISBNs: it's good to purchase your own ISBNs for your books. This way you can publish each book on any site with the same ISBN. You get ISBNs from Bowker).

You can promote to bookstores once you're set up with IngramSpark or TextStream. Theoretically, Amazon does allow you to get into that system. In reality, however, they act as the middleman, and it's too expensive for bookstores and libraries to order via Amazon. In addition, they can't return the books. Even though Amazon advertises that it has that option, it's not as effective as using IngramSpark or TextStream.

How do you promote your books?

When you know your book is in the system, contact selected bookstores directly. To set up a book signing, you can tell them you will be in town on a particular date, and you'd like to do a book signing. You tell them about your awards, and your honors, and everything you can do to bring business to them. If you can show a bookstore that with your appearance they will sell books, they will be more than happy to have you. Of course, there are some big bookstores in large places that only feature established authors.

Many smaller bookstores in smaller towns might, however, be interested in a local author. Bookstores usually love local authors. Tell them you're traveling, and you'll be in their town, and you're happy to do a book signing or a book reading. You can do all kinds of marketing to create buzz to have people arrive. Once you've done one or two, or more book signings, you can then use that as evidence that when you do a book signing, people show up. You can climb the ladder and get into bigger and bigger bookstores. You can do more book signings, and sell more and more books.

Make sure to bring enough books. You can start with a smaller number, and then figure out how many books you're selling. If you're going to a smaller venue, you will sell fewer books. If you sell just a couple of books, it's still a start, so don't get discouraged. Set up your awards and wear your medals. (I always do, and I set up so that people can see that I'm an award-winning author. If you've received a medal, wear it, as it's a great icebreaker.)

First, though, you have to be available in the IngramSpark or Baker & Taylor catalog. Then, when you make your book available via Ingram or Baker & Taylor, you need to promote it. Even though your book is there, nobody will find it if you don't push it.

Let's talk about promoting your books to libraries.

These are the two main avenues: SELF-e for e-books and LibraryBub for paperbacks.

SELF-e is a *Library Journal* platform that will let you submit your e-book, and if they like it, they will promote it to libraries for a fee.

LibraryBub is a service that will connect your paperback book with thousands of libraries via its targeted weekly newsletter. (I do have to mention that I am the founder and CEO of LibraryBub.) If you want to get your paperback into libraries, you can head over to LibraryBub and check out this service to see if it's right for you. I supervise the creation of the newsletter and send it out to more than 10,000 libraries, of which 90 percent are in the U.S. and 10 percent are in Australia, Canada, New Zealand and the United Kingdom. LibraryBub features five books in each newsletter, with information on the author, title, short blurb, cover and critical reception. To get in the newsletter, you need to be an award-winning author, a bestselling author or have been reviewed by a well-known publication, such as *Library Journal* or Readers' Favorite. If you get a positive review, such as a five-star review from Readers' Favorite, that's good enough to get into the LibraryBub newsletter.

At Leaders Press, we have a partnership with Ingram Publisher Services for sales and distribution. That's the world's largest and most reliable distribution network, combined with a sales team of passionate book lovers and access to the industry's leading e-book and POD technologies. Thanks to Ingram, we have a dedicated sales team plus 100 market reps that connect us to wherever books are being sold. We also have access to state-of-the-art warehousing and distribution.

Unfortunately, this is a partnership only traditional publishing houses and select independent houses are privileged to have, so let's talk about other ways you can get your books into stores.

Offline undisclosed locations

Before we talk about all the undisclosed locations where you can sell your books and grab the money that's lying on the table, we need to consider two things.

First is the price; the purchase of your books in these venues will depend on the price you set. You should consider offset printing for bulk purchases for the undisclosed offline locations. If you score a deal with an airport, supermarket or cruise line, you should think about offset printing rather than POD, because your margin will be much higher.

These are the main channels:

- ❑ airports;
- ❑ cruise lines;
- ❑ gift shops;
- ❑ independent bookstores;
- ❑ supermarkets.

Let's start with supermarkets. Who doesn't want to have a book in a supermarket, so you can tell your family and friends to check out the shelves in your local supermarket and get your book?

In supermarkets, fiction outsells nonfiction. For fiction authors, this is an excellent place to go. Books by local and regional authors sell, so check out if you can get your books into them as a local or regional author. Books about local and regional topics sell well too. They prefer paperbacks rather than hardbacks, as we are looking on the cheap side in supermarkets.

Indie sales are very likely. The reason why indie books are not often present in supermarkets might be because indie authors are so overwhelmed by what they see, and take it for granted that they will be denied the opportunity, so they don't even ask. If you don't ask, you're not going to get what you want!

When you get into a supermarket, you'll sell books by the thousands. You need to be aware, however, that supermarkets cut the list price by up to 25 percent, so your pricing must allow for that discount to occur profitably. Make sure you consider that when you price your book as prices below $10 are the norm. It would be best if you considered offset printing because otherwise, you won't be able to hit that low price. The books that do well in supermarkets are children's books, cookbooks, travel books and regional titles. An excellent idea for the supermarkets is a book signing. If you can convince the management that you're able to bring clients to the store via a book signing, and sell books, they will be interested in carrying your title because your business is their business.

Let's talk a bit about airports. Who doesn't want to be on those shelves? A major store in a large airport will sell between one and two million books every year. A title doesn't have to be a bestseller to find its way into the stores in large airports. Books by local and regional authors and books about travel destinations sell well in airports. Start with the airport closest to you, or if you've written about a topic that's in the area of that airport, that's also an excellent place to start. Children's books and business books do well in airports but keep in mind that paperbacks outsell hardbacks (mainly because of the weight). You must have an ISBN, a barcode and a printed price on your cover. Airports are fantastic, because not everybody has an e-reader, and even if they do, they might not have downloaded their books in time for the flight or they might prefer paper for a change. Major airport distributors include HMSHost, Paradies Lagardère and WHSmith. Send them an email, and see if they're interested. You'll need to provide a copy of your book and your terms. Your terms will include the price of your book and what their discount is going to be. Disclose the list price, but offer to sell them the books at a lower price, as the standard industry discount is 60 percent. Your marketing plan must be mentioned, and you must show them that you have it all figured out and that there will be some buzz, and people will be aware of your book before it hits the stores. You need a solid marketing plan that includes both editorial reviews and many customer reviews, so be prepared. I suggest you copy and paste two or three powerful one-liners from your reviews onto your inquiry form.

Discuss your sales history. If it's not a new book, it's a good idea to include your sales history. Even if your book is permanently free as an e-book, and has a high sales ranking on Amazon, you can boast about that. You can say, "My book has been downloaded 10,000 times." The fact that it's permanently free, and people download it, doesn't mean that it's any less desired than a $1 book. People don't download a book if they're not interested in it. There are so many free books that even the active downloading of free books itself shows that there's interest in your book.

You should also mention media coverage if you have any articles or media appearances. You don't have to be on Fox News to have good media coverage. You can mention smaller blogs, larger blogs, blog talk radio, podcasts, radio shows or short TV clips. Show that you're active, and creating buzz for your book.

Of course, include your contact information. Include it on every page for any type of document — including your manuscript — proving that it's yours. Ideally, your email should be on every page as well. Include the page count too.

Let's talk about cruise lines, which are excellent for books linked to the sea or ports of call. Contact the head of the retail department, by using LinkedIn.

Consider also contacts you might already have. You've heard about the theory of six degrees of separation — there are only six or fewer people that separate us from any given person around the world. So you probably have direct first, second or third degree access to a place where your book could sell quite well.

Keep in mind, when pitching your book, that elevator pitch we talked about based on Gary Halbert's AIDA principle (attention, interest, desire, action). You have to have that practiced because you never know when you're going to meet a person to pitch to. You need to know what you're going to say such as, "This book is for people who like cruising. The ideal age is for retired adults. It talks about ports of call. Here's your copy. I hope you enjoy it." You need to get to the point. If you get onto a cruise line, you will be selling books by the thousands. It's a perfect place to be.

Then there are gift shops and independent bookstores. Go into the store, browse around to see if there's a book in your genre. Introduce yourself and say that you're an author and that you saw that there were books that are similar to yours; that yours talks about a related subject but in a different way. It has to be unique. Ask to speak to the person responsible for stocking, or to the person from the retail department, about the possibility of carrying your books. If you can't meet with the decision maker, leave your brochure or the catalog you've prepared, and ask for their manager's contact details. Don't leave without an email contact in your hand. If you can, stop by the next time the manager's there, or if you can't, follow up by email.

Get out of your comfort zone! If speaking up is not your thing, go out there, and do it anyway. Alternatively (this is something I do at book fairs), hire a friend. If you have an outspoken friend, go with them, and let them do the talking. They can present you as the author, and act as your publicist. If you're an introvert, or if you don't like to go out and talk to people, that's the best solution!

Think of themes.

If you have a book about cars, go to gas stations, and see if they will carry your book. If you have a self-help book, contact doctors' offices or healthcare chains to have them sell it. (Make sure it fits though.) Ask them to carry it for their waiting rooms; they might be interested in having it in their library for their patients. If you have a business book, talk to multinational companies and combine that with public speaking. Make friends with higher management and try to get in by speaking. If multinational companies buy a book, they might buy a book for every employee — that could be thousands of books!

This might sound overwhelming, but you have to start somewhere. Start somewhere local, somewhere small, and document all your successes in your portfolio. Call it your media kit or success portfolio. You can go one step of the ladder higher every time.

Think out of the box.

When you're in public or browsing the Internet, think, "Will my book *fit in* here?" If you live in a big city, take a walk and try to think, "Will it *fit in* here? Will it *fit in* there?" If it doesn't *fit in*, how do you make it *fit in*? When thinking of out-of-the-box places to sell, try to be the only book. Think about situations where your book is the only book next to other merchandise. Think of places such as a beauty salon, a surf store or a farmers market.

Consider your website.

You can do anything you want on your site, and you can promote it offline. You can promote it offline via your business card. The gist here is that when you meet somebody and talk about your book, give them your business card so they know where to go to get a copy of your book. If they want to buy a paperback, consider offering it through your website, rather than through a retailer. Because even if they buy it through a retailer, your ranking will go up, but your royalties will be down. If you can sell it directly, there's no intermediary, and the royalties are all yours.

I've covered many places where you can sell your books, and there are even more places that I haven't included, but you will certainly figure that out now because you'll have your eyes open at all times!

To recap, consider the price, because when you talk to these places, you'll need to give them a 55-60 percent discount off the list price, so consider offset printing. Think themes. Get your book into alternative venues. Because if you're not doing it, you're leaving a lot of money on the table. There are a lot of new opportunities popping up every day, and we need to go out and grab them!

Where to outsource distribution

This is tough. If you go with a traditional publishing house or a hybrid publishing house, such as Leaders Press, the publisher will take care of this for you. Otherwise, you have to do it yourself by following what I described above.

An alternative would be to hire someone on Upwork or another outsourcing site, give them this chapter to read, and ask them to set up your book for distribution.

Cost

Depending on which channels you go for (making this decision is not straightforward) this could be a full time job for an assistant because pitching books to independent stores could never end! We could estimate that $1,000 a month for 12 months could do the job..

CHAPTER 13

Launch

There are hundreds of thousands of books published every year and the best way to get yours noticed is with a structured launch.

Begin by creating a launch team months before the actual launch. Engage with launch team members, and educate and motivate the group to review your book so it will launch with dozens of reviews. Those reviews will provide invaluable momentum because Amazon's algorithms will notice and promote the book further.

I'm going to break down the launch of my client's book I mentioned earlier, *Pocket Mentor*. We created the entire book for Mark Nureddine. We interviewed him. Rev transcribed his interviews. My ghostwriter wrote the book. My team promoted it to become a No. 1 bestseller. Mark didn't have to write a single word, and he's now a bestselling author!

I'll walk you through the launch so you can see how we did what we did. Everybody wants to know about launches because they're a bit of a specialty.

The first step is that one to two months before launch we scout for reviewers and create a landing page, which says "Get a free review copy before launch day on July 28" (I have a person on my team who scouts full-time for book reviewers).

On the landing page, it says, "Download your review copy here." The reader clicks and receives an automatic download of the book. I ask that he leaves a review in my Google Docs form. This is so that I can remind him what he wrote when it's time to launch. I collect his review, name and email.

Then, when the book is ready, I can say, "Hello! You wrote this review a month ago. It's launch day. Can you please copy and paste this on the book's page on Amazon?"

What I send to these readers before launch is called an advance review copy (ARC). You can write on the front page that it is unedited and unformatted, as it is an ARC. You don't want anyone to say, "Hey, this looks unedited and unformatted!" When they click to get the book, it's hooked up to my email provider, so their email goes on my list and automatically, an auto-responder is sent to them that reads, "Here's the link to the book. The launch is on July 28, and I'll keep in touch during the prelaunch time."

I set this process up one to two months before launch. This is important, as when there's a tight deadline, you send out an advance review copy which hasn't been edited or formatted because the book is with the editors during this time. In the meantime, you use that version as an ARC to get those reviewers on board. Moreover, you explain the process to set expectations.

For example, you could say, "This is not a ready book. It's an advance review copy for reviewers' eyes only," so they feel privileged because it's for their eyes only.

I divided Mark Nureddine's launch into three phases.

Phase 1 lasted four days. I released the book as a preorder at 99 cents and kept it priced that way for four days. I enrolled it in KDP Select so it's only on Amazon at first. Amazon favors the books that are enrolled in KDP select, and the trick is to start sending traffic immediately. When you publish a book on KDP, it will say that your book will be available within 72 hours, but it's usually available within 6-10 hours. When you see that it's live on Amazon, first of all, immediately buy the copy yourself, because you can buy one copy of a Kindle book. Next, send your emails to your list promoting the book, but not your launch team, because they expect to get the book for free.

I have about 20,000 subscribers (not counting librarians) on my lists. I mailed 50 percent of my business list first (I have a list of 3,000 entrepreneurs), which was on the Monday. On the Tuesday, I mailed the other half, so another 1,500 emails. On the Wednesday, I mailed half of my author list (which is about 17,000). (It was applicable because *Pocket Mentor* is about building a business and as authors we are all building a business.) On the Thursday, the book went from preorder to live. I mailed the other half of my author list. As soon as the book is live, it's no longer a preorder. I set it for free for the next day. So on the Thursday, I set in up in my KDP dashboard, so the book was free on the Friday, Saturday and Sunday. On the Thursday, I used a promo site mailing.

I don't mail the launch team in Phase 1; I only mail them in Phase 2 when the book is free. You do, however, want to have another group of people to mail, and they can come from promotional sites. Separate those people you're going to scout from your acquaintances and family members. Have the family members buy in Phase 1, and have those launch team members review in Phase 2.

Phase 2 lasts three days, during which time the book is free. You can set it for free only when it's live because you can't set a free promotion when the book is on preorder. I make the book free for the reviewers because reviewers expect to get the book for free. They've already received the book because they signed up, but I need them to download it again so that the review is verified, and this must be explained to them in your emails.

The big hit is on this last day when you want the biggest mailing. You want to have this grow because then the algorithm understands that this book is getting popular. To keep the numbers reasonable, five people buy on Day 1, 15 people buy on Day 2, 30 people buy on Day 3, 40 buy on Day 4, and more than 50 buy on Day 5. Amazon sees that your book is getting more and more popular, so that's why you want to spread out your emails throughout the launch. I didn't mail 20,000 people on the Monday. I mailed 1,500, 1,500, 8,500, 8,500, and I also used a promotion site.

I expected to rank around 10,000, yet we were at about 8,000. Then the book went live and free — and making the books free hurts the rank. During the promotion, we were one of the Top 100 most downloaded books and one of the first nonfiction books. We were at 7,000 here when we came out of the first days of the promotion, but then we were at about 40,000 after the free promo. The conclusion is that the three free days hurt the ranking, but we have to do it for the reviewers.

On the Friday, I mailed the launch team and said, "The book is out. Please download it even if you have it because when you download, it will make your review verified and it will be on top. Readers will read it and be influenced by your opinion." I share what's it in for them. You used to be able to incentivize these but you can't anymore. With the setup I have, I was able to get 100 reviews during those three days.

During Mark's launch, we got 20 reviews because of two reasons. First of all, you can't incentivize reviews. Second, the reviewers now need to have made at least $50 of purchases on Amazon. So that disqualifies many people who reviewed before. I tell the author also to tell his friends that the book is free, and they can review it, and he sees how difficult it is to get those reviews. The following Saturday, when the book was free, I mailed the launch team again. (I mailed them every day, and that gave us about 20 reviews.)

Phase 3 lasted four days. I priced Mark's book at 99 cents for the next four days. You have to promote after those free days heavily. On the Monday, I mailed my list again, and I did a promo sites mailing. On the Tuesday, I mailed my list. On the Wednesday, I used a promo site. On the Thursday, I included a link to the book in my super signature, and I will include it every week. Once the book is out, you put it in your super signature, and that's it. Soon the ranking starts to stabilize.

I also run Amazon ads, although I don't run them personally. I hired BookAds to do it. Another thing I did was to play with categories. When I saw that we were about to drop in the category in which we were listed as a No. 1 bestseller, I looked for some other categories in which we could easily rank No. 1. Playing with those categories helped and boosted the ranking. You can have up to ten categories by mailing KDP support and asking for other categories to be added to your book. Then you appear in all ten different categories.

I also use promo sites such as Bargain Booksy, Book Gorilla, Book Sends, Choosy Bookworm and Robin Reads. Some sites have criteria, such as your book has to have ten reviews, or has to have an average review of four stars. Some don't want to take preorders, but since I have a relationship with some of them, I managed to get a slot in for preorder. When the book was on preorder, I already managed to get a slot here for one of them to promote. Some sites will promote preorders without reviews; you don't have to know anybody.

What you can do is to increase the price every three weeks or so by a dollar and see how the royalties turn out. When you hit that sweet spot, for the most optimal price level, you'll keep it at that.

To recap, the new thing that I discovered and I haven't heard anybody talk about is that as soon as you see the book is live on Amazon as a preorder or as a live book, you need to send traffic immediately. That's the No. 1 takeaway.

Amazon does notice if you send traffic immediately. What I used to do in the past was similar but I didn't do preorders. I used to publish books at 99 cents, do nothing for a few days then during the free days, get the reviews and then put it back on whatever the price was supposed to be. That was a simpler strategy and it still works but the strategy we just went through is more sophisticated, advanced, effective and lucrative.

Where to outsource your book launch

While you can outsource a virtual assistant to scout for reviewers at onlinejobs.ph or timeetc.com, you need a world-class professional to orchestrate a successful book launch.

At Leaders Press, we are pros! We're a *USA Today* and *Wall Street Journal* bestselling press and we have launched every single book we've released to bestseller status. Go to outsourcemybook.com if you'd like us to take care of your book creation process and launch.

Cost

One person that I'm aware of who orchestrates book launches is Tim Grahl. I attended his webinar on bestseller lists and I believe that's where I heard him say that he charges $30,000 for a book launch..

CHAPTER 14

Bestseller Status

Becoming a bestselling author is every writer's dream. It isn't unobtainable if you know the algorithm. First, complete each step up until this point, and then add paid promotions. If you followed these steps correctly, you're almost guaranteed to achieve bestselling author status.

There are different types of bestseller status — the chief ones are *USA Today*, *Wall Street Journal* and then Amazon. It takes different strategies to attain each one.

The following is a very condensed strategy my fellow authors and I used to launch our book, *Write and Grow Rich*, to become a *USA Today* and *Wall Street Journal* bestseller.

My *USA Today* run originated in my head about a year and a half before I did anything about it. I thought it would be incredible to hit the *USA Today* list. It was in my dreams, but then I sat down with my notebook and wondered, "How could I make this dream come true?"

I knew a few things.

- ❑ I'd have to sell 6,000 books in a single week. (I've sold 100,000 books, but you have to sell 6,000 in one week.)
- ❑ Only U.S. sales count.
- ❑ I needed 500+ sales on a retailer other than Amazon.
- ❑ It must be a paid book.
- ❑ It can be a solo book or a box set.

How would I sell 6,000 books in a week? Was my list big enough to be able to pull that off? Then I started thinking about other authors I knew who might want to be involved. If we were 20 authors and we each had a list of 10,000 people, we'd have one giant list of 200,000 (okay, there would be some overlapping but not too much). Selling 6,000 books in a week would be much easier with a list like that than if I were to do it myself.

The result was that 23 authors and I hit the *USA Today* bestseller list at No. 68 out of 150 books that made the list that week. As large publishing houses mostly take those slots, independent authors are in the minority on this list. That's just one of the reasons why our ranking was such a big deal. One byproduct was that we also hit the *Wall Street Journal* list in nonfiction e-books at No. 6. Another result of this launch was that I entered the Top 100 authors in business and marketing at No. 4. I'm usually at around 50, but during this launch, I was at 4, which was pretty great. All the other authors ranked in this space as well.

It started with a dream; then there was a lot of preparation, as we figured out the requirements to hit the *USA Today* list. Each person had to create a chapter, give a bonus, contribute to ad spend, and commit that they would promote. Then, once I had that, I reached out more aggressively. When we had the team in place, we had our first obstacle with Amazon.

Before we put anything together, we received some coaching from another author who had already hit the *USA Today* list. Four or five of us got together and picked his mind for about an hour on his advice on how to orchestrate this launch.

The takeaways from this coaching call were:

- ❏ authors must be confirmed and committed to mailing;
- ❏ authors must participate in ad spend of a minimum of $500;
- ❏ you have to lock in the dates to mail;
- ❏ you have to launch on a Tuesday (which I didn't understand until I saw my sales dashboard on Amazon).

The sales for the *USA Today* week are calculated from Monday to Sunday. By launching on a Tuesday, all the preorders are calculated on the Monday before. When we launched on a Tuesday, we had 800 sales because when we launched, people bought 800 books that Tuesday. On the Monday, we had 5,000 sales, and those 5,000 sales didn't happen on one day but during the whole preorder period. They were just calculated on the Monday.

We created a promotional calendar, which looked like this.

❏ June 2	Preorder live date with June 2 and three emails to list (two mailings for a good start). Open with a few bonuses to tease extra sales.
❏ July 14	Fix algorithm and rank loss due to July 4 holiday, and new bonus introduced to keep relevance.
❏ August 4	Email with a new bonus to retain relevance and to raise sales.
❏ September 1	Email with another bonus

- ❑ September 29   On social media only, start teasing now and every couple of days until launch with mention of bonuses. Share a story to get audiences excited.
- ❑ October 2   LIVE

  Email and get as many book blogs, related blogs, affiliates and joint-venture friends as possible.
- ❑ October 3   another email and every single promo we can get
- ❑ October 4   another email and every single promo we can get

One problem I ran into was that Amazon only allows a three-month preorder period, so we decided to launch on iBooks and Barnes & Noble only, since we needed 500 sales on a platform other than Amazon, and we didn't want those sales to be diluted by using Kobo, for example.

Now that I know where the sales came from, I'd launch on iBooks only because we didn't hit the 500 at Barnes & Noble. For future sales, I'd use only Amazon and iBooks. Not being able to do a three-month preorder period on Amazon was a blessing in disguise because we managed to get the 500 sales on iBooks before we ever made the book available on Amazon! It makes sense to launch on another platform before you ever do it on Amazon, if you're going after the *USA Today* or *Wall Street Journal* bestseller lists.

On July 14, when we made the book available on Amazon, we used my three-phase launch that I described in the previous chapter. (We skipped the free period, however, because every sale counts towards hitting the lists.)

Even before Amazon sent me an email that the book was available, as soon as I saw it has been published, I mailed 8,000 of my subscribers. On July 12, I mailed another 8,000 people. On July 13, I did a Bargain Booksy feature. On July 14, all 24 authors were scheduled to mail. What I did here was build up towards this July 14 preorder launch date, which is crucial for the algorithm. The takeaway is that the Amazon algorithms immediately understood it was a popular book.

By August 7, we had 2,300 sales — 1,800 on Amazon, 526 on iBooks and 256 on Barnes & Noble. We needed 6,000 U.S. sales, and we had 60 days left. That's 3,634 sales divided by the 60 days left, or 60 sales a day. We had 6,205 on October 1, but on October 2, we had 5,800, so 400 sales were gone. What that meant is that some 400 people, or 10 percent of the buyers, had problems with their debit card or credit card. When it was time to charge their cards, they couldn't be charged so we were minus 400 sales.

We entered the launch week with 5.800 sales, out of which 5,250 were on the U.S. Amazon site. October 2 was the official launch day. We had 813 U.S. sales that day also because we had many substantial promotional pushes scheduled for then. We used promotional sites such as Book Gorilla, Buck Books and Ereader News Today. On October 3, we used even more promotional sites.

I kept mailing; I couldn't not mail. For me, October 6 and 7 were the days that still counted, so in my head, I couldn't just let go. My logic was "What if I don't mail and then we don't hit the list, and if I had mailed one more time we would've made it?" So I kept mailing. What could I do during launch week when everything was already scheduled? When I do my launches or launch for clients, there's not much to do on launch week. All the work is done before the launch. All you can do in launch week is mail, and who do you mail? You mail your list, and you mail your partners, so every day I was mailing people with updates on how many books we'd sold, and tried to sound enthusiastic to get them to mail one more time, even though they'd already mailed 10 or 20 times. During the launch, what do you do? You mail, mail, mail. That's all you can do. You mail co-authors to mail with milestone sales, and you give them swipe (the exact text they can send to their subscribers). You mail partners. You ask them to mail and you keep the Facebook group active where you communicate with your partners.

Our best recorded Amazon rank during the launch was 200. This means that *Write and Grow Rich* was the 200th most bought book on Amazon at that time. We hit No. 68 on the *USA Today* list, No. 6 on the *Wall Street Journal* list, and I got to No. 4 on the list of top business and money authors. Everybody who claimed the book arrived on this list. We pushed some huge authors way down.

What's the conclusion?

- ❏ Go after your dreams. If they seem huge, never give up; even if you've got obstacles that seem insur-mountable, never give up.

- ❏ Adjust and adapt, inspire and encourage your team, because if you're going to do this, you're going to lead the team, you're going to be the leader, you have to have a strong foundation. I think you have to be a centered and balanced person to pull this off.

❑ Get a mentor. We got some early mentoring, so I think it's essential to get a mentor. I have a mentor, an ongoing mentor that mentors me through my various ventures. It just skyrockets your career when you have somebody who mentors you.

In terms of a strategy for Amazon Best Sellers (they write it as two words), when you do everything mentioned above, you'll get there.

Write and Grow Rich required an enormous effort and I'm proud that thanks to this achievement, we can now publish authors as a *USA Today* and *Wall Street Journal* bestselling press.

We follow the three-phase launch plan, and we guarantee that your book will become a No. 1 Amazon Best Seller. Go to outsourcemybook.com to get started. We have launched all our releases to bestseller status.

Where to outsource bestseller status

Very few people actually have such niche knowledge, so there are not many experts to hire, but several of the people featured in *Write and Grow Rich* should be able to do it.

Cost

I attended Tim Grahl's webinar on bestseller lists and I believe that's where I heard him say that he charges $30,000 for a book launch that will get you to bestseller status.

CHAPTER 15

Reaching Libraries

Once you've achieved bestseller status, it will be easier to make your book available to libraries. Librarians will notice, and you can let them know yourself. Being available in libraries gives you access to millions more potential readers and clients. A survey of public libraries in the United States revealed that $1.22 billion was spent on collection expenditures, with more than 60 percent of that being spent on print materials, including books. With that much money being spent on books, what an opportunity for indie authors to get their books in libraries!

But how do indie authors rise to the top and grab the attention of librarians?

Start with the 4 Ps of marketing I describe in detail in my award-winning guide *How I Sold 80,000 Books* — product, price, promotion, place.

First, consider your **product**. It's your book, and of course, you want people to read it. Librarians have a similar goal. After all, their job is to stock their shelves with books that people want to read, and which will drive traffic into their library. As you're writing your book, consider other aspects of your book I've mentioned that make it the complete product — professional editing, the copyright page, spine/binding, and professional design, including the cover. Another item to consider is whether the book will be hardback, which tends to be more durable, or paperback, which is typically more affordable for librarians, or both.

Price your book competitively. The total purchasing power of librarians is staggering, and they all have a responsibility to make wise purchasing decisions. Moreover, you can help! When determining the price point for your book, make it competitive and offer an option to return. Also consider offering a standard industry discount, which is typically around 55 percent. If you're using a self-publishing platform such as IngramSpark or Baker & Taylor, you can set up the industry discount on your dashboard.

Spotlight your book with **promotion**. When searching for books to stock their shelves, librarians want to select books that will be popular with readers. Help librarians see that your book is popular and already in demand by securing reviews. As soon as your book is available on Amazon, set up your Author Central page. Among other things, this page will help increase your Amazon search rankings and page views. It will also be a hub for reader reviews of your book. Many librarians browse Amazon reviews before ordering books in bulk. Another type of review that librarians will search for is an editorial review. If you have a publisher, they may submit your book for review, but you can still do that yourself, and *should* do that yourself if you are self-publishing. Reach out to popular industry outlets, such as *Kirkus Reviews*, *Library Journal* and *Publishers Weekly* and ask for reviews.

Distribute your book in the right **places**. Like consumers, librarians shop for books; the difference is where librarians shop. While some will order from Amazon, most order from wholesalers such as Ingram or Baker & Taylor. I recommend that authors list their book with one of these wholesalers first to enable librarians to order in bulk from multiple publishers. Get your book listed with distributors like Ingram or Baker & Taylor.

Once your marketing strategy is implemented, here are two ways to get your book into libraries: one-by-one or en masse.

If you can help libraries get more people in the door, you'll have a better chance of having your book available for them to read. Start by connecting with the libraries in your area and let the librarians know you're willing to do a book reading or signing that will bring in your existing fans. Reference the promotional aspects you've already accomplished with your book, including your online and editorial reviews. This approach could also turn you into a local celebrity, increasing your popularity and furthering the likelihood that librarians will want to put your book on their shelves. Once you've established yourself as a local celebrity, start expanding your outreach to libraries in your county, region and state. If your success continues there, keep expanding your geographical reach.

If the one-by-one approach isn't appealing to you due to the time commitment, or if you'd prefer to reach the masses quickly, consider outsourcing this step. Hire someone from the many sites I've mentioned throughout this book to handle this promotional aspect for you. She can send emails, mailers, postcards, flyers and brochures designed to provide detailed information to a specific audience.

Another option is marketing through e-newsletters, such as LibraryBub. This service offers a feature in its weekly newsletter that is sent to thousands of librarians, helping them discover indie and small press books that they can stock in their library.

Once you've successfully marketed your book, determined the best ways to reach librarians, and secured library space for your book, you'll be well on your way to increasing exposure and gaining sales.

Where to outsource reaching libraries

Use LibraryBub, or hire an assistant.

Cost

$299 for a LibraryBub feature in a press release, and a newsletter blast to 10,000 librarians.

Hourly rates for an assistant to handle these tasks for you are from $25. Even if you had the contacts to 10,000 libraries, it would take around 500 hours to send those emails, amounting to $12,500.

CHAPTER 16

Pitching Foreign Rights

Being able to sell licensing rights to foreign publishers is next-level success. With all the hard work that's been done to get to this point, this part could seem easy. To get started, find the right agent or publisher, pitch to them, and then sell the rights and cash the check.

Every author wants to have their book published in many languages, and we usually see these big sellers on the *USA Today* list. When Dan Brown introduced his newest book, it was published in 50 languages at the same time, and that is pretty significant. You can get your book published in other languages too if you follow some of the rules we will discuss.

First, let's define what foreign rights are. You grant the rights to translate your book into a language to a particular publisher or a company for a certain time and for a certain territory. Selling foreign rights is a very easy stream of income if you do it right because the foreign publisher pays you up-front, produces your book, and translates it at their own expense, so you don't have to do anything. That's an excellent way of making additional money.

To start, you must have a website. Foreign publishers want to find out who owns the rights to the book. They need to know how to contact the author if they discover a book on their own, so they need a website to contact you. If you don't have a website yet, be sure to get one, and be accessible and respond to such inquiries.

In advance

You must know about trade shows, where you can meet people from different organizations and service companies. You will pitch your book to them at trade shows, but you will also start your research and pitches in advance of your attendance.

The Frankfurt Book Fair is the most important trade show in the world. It's the oldest and largest book fair. It's 30 times larger than the London Book Fair, for example. Publishers from all over the world gather in Frankfurt as there are about 300,000 visitors, so it's the place to sell and buy licensing rights, and it can be very fruitful if you do it right.

In general, what foreign publishers are looking for is specific material that hasn't been published in their market yet; something cutting edge that hasn't been done before. Your homework would be to study the publisher and see if there is something similar on their site. If you're not well known and you don't have a robust platform, it's going to be much more difficult. You don't want to waste the publisher's time because they're busy. That's why it's good to make an appointment ahead of time after checking out this publisher's website and determining that you're a good fit. So contact them ahead of time. You can go to the Frankfurt Book Fair's website and see the list of publishers who will be attending. Contact the publishers in advance and find out if they would be interested in seeing your material. Be prepared to give them a small, short pitch, which you have prepared in advance, and follow their submission guidelines. Write to them and see if they're interested. If you contact enough people, you may find someone who is willing to meet you if your material is appropriate for them. It's like fishing. You put out your bait and eventually you will get something; however, it's a lot of work, and you have to be persistent and patient.

You have to practice your pitch. It has to be short, like an elevator pitch. Include one center topic, a bit about you, and then you can tell them a bit about the content. I suggest you follow the AIDA framework (attention, interest, desire, action). You want to grab the person's attention. You need to go deeper so that they show interest. Then you want to have them desire what you have. For example, you can mention awards, if they're strong. Finally, you present a call to action to make them do something.

If you study the publisher's submission guidelines, they will generally want a query, which has to be very short. If they're interested, they'll contact you and ask for more. Tell them how many copies you sold because every publisher wants to buy a product that has already sold. The more books you have sold, the better.

What to bring

When meeting with professionals, one significant thing is to have something to hand out to them so they remember you, such as a flyer or a business card with your email and address. Give them what you have, and then continue the conversation by email later on. If you have several titles, you need a catalog. Don't print it on heavy-duty paper. You just need a short list of the books, as you have to carry it around the book fair.

Walk the aisles and look around. It's essential that you scout and see what other authors are writing. You can look for distributors, for example.

At the fair

Walk the aisles and talk to the people at the different booths. Give them your short pitch. Hear what they have to say about your book. Everybody will be friendly and give you at least some advice, although people are often very busy at these shows, and time is precious.

For example, you can learn if your book can travel. If you pitch your book to these foreign publishers or agents, they may see your book may not work for them, but it may work in South America. It might work for the Spanish readers, but not for the agent's culture. There are substantial differences in cultures. You would have to adapt your material depending on where it would fit best.

Usually, only very famous and bestselling authors will be translated into other languages. If, however, you have an active list or some cutting-edge ideas, you always have a chance. It has to be a unique book on a unique topic. If, though, your topic is timeless, you still have a chance to find a publisher even many years afterwards.

The publishers are also looking for your platform. They're interested to see that you have a following on social media, that you're a great promoter, and that your background qualifies you as an expert on your material.

A book that's been out for many years has a chance. It depends on how it *fits in* with the specific publisher's program and profile. In general, they like to look at new material, even unpublished material. If they think it would be successful in their country, you could get an offer even if your book is not published.

In those cases, the foreign publishers would like to have you present in their country and help promote the book. Let's say you're dealing with an Italian publisher. If you can spend some time in Italy, or maybe you know the language, they would like you to be there and help them with the marketing of the book; that would be helpful. All the things that you do here can be done in other countries, in other languages, as well.

Publishers invest a lot of money into each book they take on. A translation costs a lot, as they pay translators per word. They put in money up-front to get the translation right, and they also pay you on the print run of however many copies they agree to print. What they seek must match their profile. You often don't know what they are going to publish next year until you look at their program.

Consider the territories. Perhaps a children's book will sell in China because the Chinese learn English from kindergarten. They are very interested in English; there might be no need for translation. There are all kinds of possibilities that you can pursue at a trade show.

Every country wants bestsellers. That's paramount. If your book is on the *USA Today* bestseller list, you as an author can lean back, and they will likely jump on it, and you'll get swamped with inquiries. The more books you sell domestically, the better it is for your foreign rights deals.

Your homework after the fair

When returning from the book fair, the work begins as you have to do something with all your leads. Many people just put this folder or their notes aside and forget about it. You have to work on your leads and follow up with these people that you met. Send them what they wanted. Contact them kindly. Push a little bit, but not too hard, if you don't get an answer right away it's because everybody who participates will get tons of emails afterwards. Agents have to go through them and sort them, store them, and see what to do with the material. It's hectic and very intense after a trade show.

If you don't get an answer, be patient. It can take up to a half a year before publishers work their way through all the requests and material after a trade show. Spend your time preparing new PR for your book or new awards to share with your foreign partners. Send them reviews, but don't send too many attachments or big files. Anything that happens on media is significant to share with the foreign agent. Of course, submit your sales numbers. If they go up, that's another big thing. It would be best if you always told them about that.

A year later, if you haven't heard from your leads, don't give up. You can try again. If, however, you do find a publishing house, stay close. Build a relationship with them and find out what they're publishing. Know their program for the upcoming year and for the upcoming season. You have to be aware of the cultural differences, so sometimes communication is an issue. Many foreign publishers and agents are not fluent in English. Sometimes what you get as a message may not be entirely clear, so you have to kind of guess what they're meaning. Staying updated is important. If you want to go to the next trade show, you want to have everything handy so that you don't have to go through tons of scattered notes. Stay organized.

If you want to sell translation rights to your book, make sure you have all the extra material for your book. Have it ready because it's very valuable — the publisher will buy it and use their translation. Often they will exchange the language and use all the layout and images and plug the text in, so everything has to be organized and available. Stock photos can be a tricky area as they're often limited to a specific territory. If you want a foreign publisher, make sure they can use them, or they will be fined by the stock photo company.

When you receive a "Yes"

Assuming that you receive a go, learn how to negotiate an excellent deal for your book. If you can, always start with an agent who specializes in translation rights licensing because this agent will walk you through the whole process and help you negotiate an excellent deal for your book.

You should be familiar with some of the terms. There are terms, such as the language the book should be translated into and the territory, which is the geographical area of the deal.

There can be some sensitivities around different genres. For example, some Asian countries won't resonate with your material. Religious topics are a little sensitive. Some topics travel very well because they are new or exotic or haven't been published yet. You can never say never. There's always a chance.

The German language usually is for Germany, Austria and Switzerland. The Spanish language has Spain and also America. We can have two deals. We sell a book to a Spanish publisher for Spain, or we can have a publisher in South America who wants to have Spanish rights for South America. Alternatively, we can have a large publisher who wants all the Spanish rights which include South America and Spain and all other Spanish-speaking countries around the world. The same applies to rights. There's the territory of Mainland China which has Chinese Simplified for their territory. There's Taiwan and some other territories who want the translation to be in complex Chinese characters. Those are particular things. There's Portuguese in Portugal, Portuguese in Brazil and Portuguese worldwide.

We usually deal with translation rights with e-books, and they are typically included in most of these territories nowadays. Every country has e-books, but some are not as strong as here; however, usually, the publishers would also want to include e-book rights if they buy your translation rights.

Let's talk about the art of negotiations. It sounds a little dry, and I think it's better to get to it when you have a deal or if you have an offer, but you should learn all about it. There is a limit to the contract, there are royalties due, and there's a royalty advance payment defined in the agreement.

We can calculate this royalty advance based on the retail price and the print runs the foreign publishers are planning. For example, if the publisher plans to print 2,000 copies from their translation and the book will cost $10 per copy, we normally charge 6 percent royalties on the retail price. You're going to take 6 percent of $10, and multiply this by the 2,000 copies the publisher will print. 6 percent of $10 multiplied by 2,000 = $1,200 (a small advance). That would be typical for smaller countries. It also depends on the publisher's marketing capabilities, their size and how many copies they think they can sell in one year. If they say they can only sell 2,000 maximum in one year, you can try to negotiate with them and ask them to bump it up a little bit. Part of the negotiation is trying to get more of course. It's not very much money so you could aim for $1,500 or $2,000. If this is all this publisher can do, however, you might want to take it.

The art of negotiation also means that each party has to be happy with the deal. You cannot just ask for a huge amount of money. You will disappoint the foreign publisher, and they will walk away. Consider their economic situation. You want them to market the book. They have to have some money left to promote your book and to make it a successful title. In between those numbers, we can work out a deal that satisfies both parties. You can give this foreign publisher a chance and see what happens. If they're successful, you'll get more money in the year after, hopefully, and you get your annual royalty statements and possibly royalty payments in the future. You can make a lot of money, but also you can make very little money and have your book translated into many languages; it's all negotiable. Of course, bestselling books will make big money, and publications that are not so well known will make some money, but of course, not in that range. Usually, it's between $1,500 and $3,000. Some good deals amount to $5,000.

Where to outsource pitching foreign rights

I have a masterclass where you can learn about foreign rights, and also submit your book to my agent at sellforeignrights.com. You could outsource active pitching of the book to foreign publishers to a virtual assistant or a publicist.

Cost

It's going to be a percentage of your book sales. If you were to hire a virtual assistant or a publicist to pursue foreign rights, you'd have to pay them a full salary, say $1,000 a month for 12 months.

CHAPTER 17

Your Sales Funnel

Book royalties are great, but you'll almost always generate more revenue on the back end than on the front.

Surprised?

For example, the e-book version of *How I Sold 80,000 Books* is free, but that doesn't mean I make zero dollars on it. The free book is the front end to my six-figure sales funnel. The first step in getting this set up is ensuring your sales funnel is in place the moment you publish your book.

If you're ready to expand your skills and share your business expertise as an author, follow the steps I've discussed in previous chapters to increase your visibility and become a bestselling author.

Traditional publishing houses want you to think that you need them, and only them, to be successful. I'm here to tell you, however, that they're wrong and I have many examples to prove this. If you ever thought that traditional publishers want you to fail, you're probably right. They don't benefit from you succeeding. How many times have you seen a link to the publisher's website in a book but no link to the author's website? That's just one example. The difference with me is that I actually care about your success, and genuinely want to see you living the life of your dreams.

I know you have a dream to change people's lives with the words you've written, and I want to show you how to make that happen. The only way for you to build a successful author business is through a funnel. Moreover, the only way to create a funnel that works is through a proven model.

I'll mention again that I'm a *USA Today* and *Wall Street Journal* bestselling author, and that I've received multiple awards and sold more than 80,000 books. What's essential for you to know is that I sold rights to 16 book titles, and have more in the pipeline. I've got more than 1,000 Amazon reviews. And I have several six-figure funnels in place (that's a big factor).

Now, I have to tell you that I wasn't always in demand as a book-marketing coach. I remember when I launched one of my first books back in 2011, I was so excited about my book's release that day; I went out with my then boyfriend (and now husband) to celebrate the book launch. That was before you carried the phone with you all the time; at least before I did. When we returned home, I went online to check how many copies I'd sold. I was pretty excited about what I thought I'd see. When I saw that I didn't sell anything, I was so disappointed. I couldn't believe it. I couldn't believe that nobody bought what I thought was such a splendid book.

Immediately, I knew that I had to let readers know that my book existed! That's when I started trying every possible thing to make sales. If you keep trying, you eventually succeed. I did make a few sales, but then, when I was launching my second book, the same thing happened. I didn't have any means to tell the people who already bought Book 1 to buy Book 2. When readers found me and bought the book, that was the end of their journey with me. So I thought, "How awesome would it be if I had my readers' email addresses? I could email them about my new releases, instead of waiting to be discovered." I started wondering how I could get people to give me their emails, and that's how, without even knowing it, I began to build my very first funnel. When I launched my subsequent book, I already had a modest following and was able to launch with a substantial number of reviews, and hit the bestseller charts.

Recently, using this same method, we hit the *USA Today* and the *Wall Street Journal* bestseller lists with *Write and Grow Rich*.

Now I'm able to create funnels, which is also one of the reasons that you are reading this book. You're going through a funnel that I created that you can emulate to gain readers and potentially clients.

I'll show you how to do that.

You probably want to launch your book to bestseller status too, but maybe you have a non-existent or very limited following, so launching a book with a bang is hard. You have no control over what people do once they've read your book. A funnel makes your author business lucrative because you're leading your reader down a precisely defined path to the point that you're able to predict your income from each subscriber. Then it becomes like a vending machine.

With a vending machine, you know precisely what pops out when you put in a coin. You're able to identify the lifetime value of your subscriber; then it's effortless to make predictions, any financial predictions. So that's something you want to create — a business that's a vending machine, and I'll show you how to do that.

Secret No. 1 we already talked about in a previous chapter, which is creating a successful book idea. You can write a book that will sell, even if you've never done it before. Even though there are millions and millions of books, not everything has been done, and you can come up with a unique selling proposition. Even if you already have a book out, it's not too late because you can always reposition it, and then relaunch it.

Secret No. 2 is to launch your book with a bang so that you can ride Amazon's algorithm. We also talked about the launch in a previous chapter, so you're good to go there.

Secret No. 3 is how to turn your reader into a lifetime buyer and launch your six-figure funnel.

Case Study No. 1

I wrote the Maya and Filippo series that I mentioned in an earlier chapter. The first book in the series is permanently free on Amazon. Inside the book, readers are invited to go to a landing page, leave their email address, and get another free book. So they get two free books. That's quite generous. You might be cringing right about now, especially if you haven't written a book yet or if you've only written one book. These books, however, don't have to be huge in volume.

The lead generator — the freebie they get from your website — doesn't have to be a book. It can be a spreadsheet if you're writing a business or nonfiction book. You can give away a checklist of important steps to take or something along those lines. Just make sure it's something of value to the reader.

For fiction writers, it can be a short prequel to your bigger book that's maybe 30 pages long. It doesn't even have to be long. When people sign up for the lead generator, they have no idea how fat or thin it is. You offer a freebie to get the person's email and be able to engage with them. There always has to be value delivered, but you can provide the value in 30 pages instead of 300 pages.

Why do this?

When someone signs up for the free stuff, they are expressing interest in your books. You can then engage with them and offer them all your other books. With this strategy, if you're writing fiction, you will see a more substantial and more significant return on investment. The more books you write, the more products you have to offer, and the more lucrative this process becomes.

With your books, you can create a package and sell it from your website. You don't have to be technologically advanced as you only need a PayPal button. It doesn't have to be an automatically generated thing with a membership site that's behind a password. You don't need to make it complicated.

All you need is a PayPal link, and then when you're at your computer, email your book or book bundle as a PDF. It can be done easily at first. It doesn't have to be very techy. You can do that later. Get started easily, but do get started.

The more books you have in a series, the more lucrative it becomes. For example, I sold rights to a Chinese publisher who wanted the books because they were all part of a series. When a publisher buys foreign rights, they pay per book. As you know now, it's a specific amount that they pay per book. This publisher bought rights to 15 books, and that was a sizeable sale for me at the time.

Case Study No. 2

My book, *How I Sold 80,000 Books*, is free on Amazon. It's well-positioned, and it's optimized for online sales. It's important to do that. When somebody opens it, they are invited to sign up for a mini-course when they go to the website, so that's one of the ways people end up on my list.

After that, I engage with my subscribers, and there's a lot that I offer, as I strive to provide much value:

- ❑ I have a summit.
- ❑ I have a mastermind.
- ❑ There's LibraryBub, where I connect authors with librarians.
- ❑ I also have a high-end, done-for-you publishing service.

Case Study No. 3

I offer something unique. I write the Supreme Leadership series where I invite high-profile influencers and business leaders to be interviewed for books. Now, that's free. In the end, however, we ask if they're interested in having their book written. A percentage are interested.

It doesn't take too many people to make this particular funnel hit six figures. I mention this to show you how creative you can be with these funnels, and how many different things you can do. Your book is your ultimate business card, and when positioned and launched correctly, it can be the entrance to your world and to a lucrative funnel.

Where to outsource pitching foreign rights

It all comes down to coming up with a smart lead generator and a clear call to action. At Leaders Press, this is something we do for every author.

Otherwise, it's something you should deliver in-house or together with your ghostwriter. In order to put the tech together, I recommend Ciprian Soleriu of untasks. co, who automated a lot of my own processes.

Cost

This will be a matter of creating the content with your ghostwriter, and setting up the tech. It would probably cost a few thousand dollars.

THE BIG REVEAL

Where to Outsource Each Piece of the Book Creation Puzzle

I must admit creating this guide has been a fun exercise for me, and I trust it contains beneficial information for you.

To sum up, these are all the places to consider to get your book ghostwritten, published and launched.

Where to outsource positioning

This is a tricky one because it requires vast knowledge of the market in your particular genre. I'm confident to say that most of the authors whom I invited to be co-authors of *Write and Grow Rich* should be able to help. Their details are given below.

Where to outsource an outline

Credo, Fiverr, FreeeUp, Freelancer, Hubstaff Talent, Outsourcely, PeoplePerHour, Textbroker, Upwork, Workhoppers

Where to outsource getting ideas out of your head

Credo, Fiverr, FreeeUp, Freelancer, Hubstaff Talent, Outsourcely, PeoplePerHour, Textbroker, Upwork,

Workhoppers

Where to outsource transcription

Rev

Where to outsource developmental editing

Editorial Freelancers Associations, Fiverr, Independent Editors Group, Kibin, Kirkus Editorial, Postscripting, Preditors & Editors, Readers' Favorite, Scribendi, Upwork

Where to outsource copy editing

Editorial Freelancers Associations, Fiverr, Independent Editors Group, Kibin, Kirkus Editorial, Postscripting, Preditors & Editors, Readers' Favorite, Scribendi, Upwork

Where to outsource layout and formatting

AtRiteX

Where to outsource a cover

Damonza, Fiverr, 99designs

Where to outsource optimizing your book for online sales

Many of my co-authors of *Write and Grow Rich* (listed below) have solid knowledge on this.

Where to outsource a captivating book description

CopyChief is a website for business owners and entrepreneurs who want to hire copywriters. You'll be able to find, vet, and hire seasoned copywriters with a proven track record. Another source is conversionengineering.co where my fellow mastermind member can improve both your book description and any other copy for your business so that you increase your conversions.

Where to outsource an outstanding bio

CopyChief

Where to outsource distribution

This is tough. If you go with a traditional publishing house or a hybrid publishing house, such as Leaders Press, the publisher will take care of this for you. Otherwise, you have to do it yourself by following what I described above. An alternative would be to hire someone on Upwork or another outsourcing site, give them this book to read, and ask them to set up your book for distribution.

Where to outsource your book launch

While you can outsource a virtual assistant to scout for reviewers at onlinejobs.ph or timeetc.com, you need a world-class professional to orchestrate a successful book launch. At Leaders Press, we are pros! We're a USA Today and Wall Street Journal bestselling press and we have launched every single book we've released to bestseller status. Go to outsourcemybook.com if you'd like us to take care of your book creation process and launch.

Where to outsource bestseller status

Very few people actually have such niche knowledge, so there are not many experts to hire, but several of the people featured in Write and Grow Rich should be able to do it. I've also heard that Tim Grahl can orchestrate launches.

Where to outsource reaching libraries

Use LibraryBub, or hire an assistant.

Where to outsource pitching foreign rights

I have a masterclass where you can learn about foreign rights, and also submit your book to my agent at sellforeignrights. com. You could outsource active pitching of the book to foreign publishers to a virtual assistant or a publicist.

Where to outsource the facilitation of your sales funnel

It all comes down to coming up with a smart lead generator and a clear call to action. At Leaders Press, this is something we do for every author. Otherwise, it's something you should deliver in-house or together with your ghostwriter. In order to put the tech together, I recommend Ciprian Soleriu of untasks.co, who automated a lot of my own processes.

Check out these co-authors of the bestselling *Write and Grow Rich* from Leaders Press. Many of them provide outsourcing options for aspects of your book.

Steve Alcorn http://bit.ly/writing-academy-publishing

Alexa Bigwarfe writepublishsell.co

Lise Cartwright www.hustleandgroove.com

Bryan Cohen www.BryanCohen.com

Amy Collins www.newshelves.com

Claire Diaz-Ortiz www.clairediazortiz.com

Derek Doepker www.BestsellerSecrets.com

Debbie Drum debbiedrum.com

Susan Friedmann http://avivapubs.com

Marc Guberti marcguberti.com

Daniel Hall danielhallpresents.com

Adam Houge www.thefanbaseformula.com

Christine Kloser www.christinekloser.com

Donna Kozik www.FreeBookPlanner.com

Jason Ladd www.jasonbladd.com

Kristen Joy Laidig www.KristenJoysBlog.com

Sally Miller www.sallyannmiller.com

Derek Murphy www.creativindie.com

Kirsten Oliphant createifwriting.com

Caitlin Pyle caitlinpyle.co

Jyotsna Ramachandran
www.happyselfpublishing.com

Matt Stone www.100covers.com

Summer Tannhauser summertannhauser.com

Cost

This is the cost you're looking at when you outsource every aspect of book creation.

Positioning This could probably be done in a 60-minute strategy call = approximate cost $600.

Outline With an experienced ghostwriter and some ideas of your own, you should be able to put it together in 90 minutes. The approximate cost of interviewing time, transcription and writing is $500.

Getting ideas out of your head You could probably get away with $1,500 for the interviewing and transcription of the 50,000-word example book mentioned above, but this doesn't include the actual writing which comes next.

Transcription The average cost for transcription is $1 per minute. I've found the math to approximate a 1:3 structure, meaning for every hour of speaking, there will be three hours of transcribing.

Ghostwriting When you shop around online, you'll find that depending on the source, quality and book length, the fees for ghostwriting generally range between $18,000 and $150,000+. The range in talent varies as much as the range in prices!

Developmental editing At around $.08 per word, it would amount to $4,000 for a 50,000-word book.

Copy editing At around $.018 per word, it would amount to $900 for a 50,000-word book.

Layout and formatting for simple text probably around $200

Cover between $5 to $1,000

Optimizing your book for online sales It should be possible to optimize your book for online sales during a 60-minute coaching call. That costs about $600.

Book description I think you should be able to get it done for $300-$1,000 but that might be a significant underestimation. In some cases, copywriters will require a percentage of royalties.

Bio $300-$1,000

Distribution Depending on which channels you go for (making this decision is not straightforward) this could be a full time job for an assistant because pitching books to independent stores could never end! We could estimate that $1,000 a month for 12 months could do the job.

Launch Tim Grahl charges $30,000 for a book launch.

Bestseller status A book launch by Tim Grahl is designed to get you to bestseller status.

Reaching libraries $299 for a LibraryBub feature in a press release, and a newsletter blast to 10,000 librarians. Hourly rates for an assistant to handle these tasks for you are from $25. Even if you had the contacts to 10,000 libraries, it would take around 500 hours to send those emails, amounting to $12,500.

Pitching foreign rights It's going to be a percentage of your book sales. If you were to hire a virtual assistant or a publicist to pursue foreign rights, you'd have to pay them a full salary, say $1,000 a month for 12 months.

Facilitation of your sales funnel This will be a matter of creating the content with your ghostwriter, and setting up the tech. It would probably cost a few thousand dollars.

In total, you're looking at $85,704 (using the lowest fees I quoted) — and you have to manage the whole endeavor!

As an alternative, allowing you to **outsource the full process** of your book creation is what we do at Leaders Press.

The authors we work with are usually CEOs and presidents of companies with many years of experience.

I created this book as a tool for both lead generation and lead conversion.

It works as a tool for lead generation because when you search on Google or on Amazon "how to get your book ghostwritten" or something to that effect, it pops up (because it's been positioned well), and seduces you to get it with its attention grabbing title, attractive cover and professionally written description.

It's also a great tool for lead conversion because it's the perfect book for me to offer to potential authors who are looking into working with Leaders Press but want to be more familiar with the process and with what we deliver. As a result, I'm looking forward to creating a similar tool for lead generation and lead conversion for you and your business!

Go to outsourcemybook.com and let's see if we're a good fit to work together!

AFTERWORD

What You Didn't Know about This Book

I think you'll find it amusing that I've outsourced the writing of this book. I simply gave my best writer links and scripts to various webinars, masterminds and articles that I've already created, asked her to fill in the blanks and presto — just like magic — this book has been done!

I'm marketing it like every other Leaders Press new release — to become a #1 Amazon Best Seller. If you think about it, getting your book outsourced with Leaders Press is very easy. You talk, we get your book done.

These are just some of the benefits of getting your book idea out of your head and launching it with a bang:

❑ authority — establishes you as the expert in your arena;

❑ visibility — customers, CEOs, business people around the world will know who you are;

❑ credibility — a book is the new calling card for your company;

❑ financial — a properly marketed book is a cash-generating asset (Yes, even one book!);

❑ invitation — top-ranked books provide many readers with an entrance into your world;

❑ popularity — books open the door to speaking gigs;

- ❑ consultancy — to be a consultant in semi-retirement, a book is a perfect method to get there;

- ❑ legacy — explain to your family and heirs just what you did when you were not at home;

- ❑ ease — all of the above just happens without you having to write the book yourself!

I'd love to work with you.

Go to outsourcemybook.com and let's see if we're a good fit to work together!